Praise for *Toxic*

"I'll be forever changed by *Toxic Positivity* ... before offering words of validation, I will choose what I say wisely. Whitney Goodman's book unlocks the difference between being helpful and harmful. This trailblazing book will help you transform your perspective about positivity."

—Nedra Glover Tawwab, bestselling author of
Set Boundaries, Find Peace

"Sorely needed . . . Whitney Goodman elegantly weaves together her personal and clinical experience, academic research, and practical advice to offer us a refreshing antidote to the seemingly innocuous but ultimately harmful message of 'good vibes only.'"

—Iris McAlpin, trauma professional

"Whitney Goodman's *Toxic Positivity* is a much-needed breath of fresh air in the self-help space. It's the validation we've all been needing in order to fully understand the normal challenges that accompany our lives."   —Todd Baratz, LMHC, psychotherapist

"Living an authentic life means facing hard times and growing through them, not pretending things are perfect when they're not. This book provides a much-needed road map for being honest with ourselves and others in order to be truly present in our own lives and grow as a whole person."

—Scott Barry Kaufman, PhD, host of
The Psychology Podcast and author of *Transcend*

"Finally a book that explains exactly why 'positivity at all costs' backfires, and teaches us how to process our pain instead of pretending it doesn't exist. *Toxic Positivity* is the antidote to superficial pop-psychology inspo, illustrating the limits of positive thoughts and gratitude, encouraging us to embrace life's ups and downs, and giving us more realistic and helpful ways to implement 'positivity.' Funny isn't, it? Stop chasing happiness and you may end up a little . . . happier."   —Caroline Dooner, author of *Tired as F*ck*

"If you've ever felt like something is wrong with you because you're having a hard time and can't seem to 'just get over it,' this book will help you understand why. Moreover, *Toxic Positivity* teaches you what to do when witnessing the struggles of others—it will help you to be a better friend, parent, colleague, or partner when someone you love is having a difficult time. This book is the counterbalance to a world that preaches 'look on the bright side' whenever life gets tough."

—Elizabeth Earnshaw, LMFT, relationship expert
and author of *I Want This to Work*

TOXIC POSITIVITY

....

*Keeping It Real
in a World Obsessed with
Being Happy*

Whitney Goodman

A TarcherPerigee Book

TarcherPerigee
an imprint of Penguin Random House LLC
penguinrandomhouse.com

Most TarcherPerigee books are available at special quantity discounts for bulk
purchase for sales promotions, premiums, fundraising, and educational needs.
Special books or book excerpts also can be created to fit specific needs. For
details, write SpecialMarkets@penguinrandomhouse.com.

Hardcover ISBN: 9780593418277
Ebook ISBN: 9780593418284
Trade paperback ISBN: 9780593542750

Printed in the United States of America
1st Printing

Book design by Tiffany Estreicher

For my husband.
In good times and bad times, I choose you.

Contents

You Deserve More Than Just Good Vibes

I would bet there are three potential reasons why you picked up this book:

1. You've been impacted by toxic positivity and are sick of it.

2. You don't know what toxic positivity is, but you're intrigued.

3. You have no idea how positivity could *possibly* be toxic, and you're determined to find out what absolute blasphemy I'm spewing in this book.

No matter what your reason is, I'm really glad you're here.

Like many aspiring therapists, I got into the field for reasons I didn't fully understand at the time. I knew I liked helping people, and I was obsessed with learning about their stories. But I would later discover (through the help of my therapist) that I actually wanted to get into the profession because I thought if I learned everything about relationships and the human psyche, I could fix everyone I loved and never feel pain again. Fellow therapists and future therapists, I know you get me here.

So I entered the field wide-eyed and delusional. I was closed off and hardened. I wanted my clients to be vulnerable without having to be so myself. I thought I would fix people, but no one needed fixing; they just needed to be heard and supported. I thought I would be the all-knowing speaker, but I'm the listener. I thought I would understand myself and the world, but now I have more questions. I thought I'd change everyone around me; instead, I learned the only person I could change was myself. My motivations for entering the field may have been a little off, but wow, I'm glad I'm here.

I love being a therapist, and I've always felt a little rough around the edges among my colleagues. I've never been a meditating, tea-drinking, yoga type of therapist. My voice is too loud, I don't wear cardigans, and I hate all the "inspirational" quotes on the walls. I tried to make myself softer. I tried to get into the affirmations and all those interventions that tell you to "get in touch with your inner child and show it love." I couldn't do it. That's how I've felt reading most of the self-help and psychology books out there. They all feel really soft and gentle. I want someone to tell it like it is and to be honest. I had a bit of an identity crisis as a new therapist, and it wasn't until I started posting my thoughts on Instagram as @sitwithwhit that I realized there was value in how I wanted to show up.

On February 1, 2019, I was scrolling on Pinterest and saw so many self-help and "inspirational" quotes being shared thousands of times. The bright colors and whimsical fonts made me irritated. I felt dismissed and concerned for anyone who might see these while in a fragile state. I started a Pinterest board of "happiness" and "inspirational" quotes that bothered me, and have continued collecting them over the years. (That board actually served as the inspiration for the cover of this book.) That same day, I shared one of my first charts on Instagram, listing some of those quotes from Pinterest, referring to them as "toxic positivity," and providing some alternative statements that I thought offered more validation and hope. This was my first "viral" post, and my tiny following multiplied in the wake of sharing this chart. I was shocked by how many people agreed with my perspective and how the phrase *toxic positivity* resonated. It was also the first time I dealt with significant criticism and pushback online from people who disagreed with my perspective. I have continued creating toxic positivity posts on grief, racism, and other important topics over the last several years, and they are some of my most popular and controversial posts to date. I knew I was on to something but never could've imagined just how much this topic would resonate with others.

Toxic positivity is something that I have been aware of for a long time but didn't have a name for. I saw it in my own home growing up, all over social media, at religious services, in school, and eventually as a therapist, with my clients. It was something that I noticed we were all contributing to, but behind closed doors everyone was telling me they hated it. I was doing it, too; it felt like I had to be a part of it or I would be considered "negative." It had woven its way into my professional and personal life; once I noticed it, it was hard to look away.

I may have just noticed this phenomenon, but the truth is, it's been around for centuries. Scholars, journalists, and researchers like Sara Ahmed, Audre Lorde, Barbara Ehrenreich, Gabriele Oettingen, and bell hooks have long been critical of the relentless pursuit of happiness and have eloquently uncovered its destructive nature throughout the world, especially within marginalized communities. Their works were instrumental in helping me understand how pervasive toxic positivity has become. Despite an abundance of research on the ineffectiveness of positivity in various situations, the self-help community continues to push positivity and the pursuit of happiness at every turn. I wanted to find a way to bring this research out of the academic ivory tower and into the modern world.

My clients and my personal life are the true inspiration for this book and the reason it exists. This career has afforded me the privilege of sitting in a room with zero distractions and getting to know people on a profound level every single day. It's an experience like no other, and it has taught me so much about life, the world, and human nature. Every single client has changed me in some way. I am eternally grateful for the humanity, struggle, and perseverance I have witnessed and continue to witness within those walls. I've taken different stories from my years as a therapist and combined them with research on positive thinking, emotions, relationships, and motivation to help you understand how positivity can become toxic and what to do instead. All identifying details have been changed to maintain the anonymity of my clients. I hope these stories will help you feel a little bit less alone and show you just how many other people are feeling the way you feel.

This is a book I've been writing on Instagram and in my office for years without knowing. It's honest, authentic, and real. It's a book for people who want to know how they can support themselves and others. It's for people who are exhausted from pretending to be happy all the time—at work, at home, with their friends, and on social media. They're tired of good vibes being forced on them at every turn and being told everything happens for a reason. I wrote this book for the people who haven't been able to manifest the perfect life. I wrote it for the humans with too many feelings and too many thoughts. I wrote it for me, and I wrote it for you.

Happiness and positivity have become both a goal and an obligation. At every turn, we're told that we need to be grateful or more positive. If something goes wrong in your life, it's because you had a "bad attitude" or you "didn't try hard enough." I'm in awe of the ways toxic positivity has woven its way into so many aspects of our lives. We see it in the workplace, in our homes, and in our relationships. It's also a powerful force that helps maintain sexism, racism, homophobia, transphobia, ableism, classism, and other types of prejudice. It really is *everywhere*.

I combed through everything we know about this history of positive thinking and the research on how we can do better and live better. I wanted this book to be easy to read and understand while also being extremely practical. *Toxic Positivity* is divided into nine chapters, and each chapter touches on a different client's story and relationship with toxic positivity. If you're interested in a comprehensive look at toxic positivity, how it impacts us, and what to do instead, I recommend reading the book cover to cover. For those of you who want to get down to the how-tos, feel free to skip to the chapters that speak to your specific need and experience.

Positive thinking has been packaged and sold as the cure to all our problems. From *good vibes only* bumper stickers to scroll after scroll of prettily designed Instagram affirmations to Life Is Good T-shirts and gurus promising you're only one positive thought away from happiness, we are consistently told that "looking on the bright side" will help us avoid difficult experiences and feelings. This book might make you feel something other than joy or happiness or good vibes. It might shine a light on habits or phrases that have become part of your daily vernacular. It might make you uncomfortable. I hope it makes you think and reconsider all the ways that you may be suppressing your own emotions and needs in the name of happiness. I hope it makes you think about all the ways you've made yourself smaller or more palatable in pursuit of good vibes. I hope it helps you express your needs and develop relationships based on more than just a good time.

If this book allows you to make room in your life for the good, the bad, and the ugly, I've done my job.

Just Be Positive!

If it were that easy or effective, we'd all be doing it. Allow yourself to experience what it means to be a human—the good and the bad.

Chapter One

What Is Toxic Positivity?

I magine that you just lost your job. You're in full panic mode. Your mind is racing, and you have no idea what you're going to do next.

You decide to share this with a friend. They glance your way and smile. It looks like they are keying up to tell you something big. Could this be the validation you need right now? Maybe they know of a great job opportunity? You watch them fidget as they pull from the depths of their inner wisdom and say, "At least you have all this time off now! It could be so much worse. Think about how much you're going to learn from this."

Toxic positivity has officially entered the building.

You freeze and think, *Are they even listening to me? Am I seriously supposed to be grateful that I just lost my job?*

You're not sure where to go from here. You don't feel grateful, so how in the world are you supposed to respond? You were already stressed out, and now this conversation leaves you feeling totally misunderstood. So, you put aside your feelings and say, "Yeah, thanks."

Now you're not only jobless, but you also feel distant from your friend and ashamed that you can't just look on the bright side.

They're Just Trying to Help

Listen, this person probably has good intentions. What they said isn't false—you WILL have more time off now, and of course things could (always) be worse, and yes, you'll likely learn some lessons from the experience.

The problem is, you're not there yet. You're still worried and upset. You're scared. Your body and mind are in full crisis mode, and no platitude is going to change that. What you really need is support and space to sort through your feelings.

Toxic positivity is the advice we might technically want to integrate but are incapable of synthesizing at the moment. Instead, it typically leaves us feeling silenced, judged, and misunderstood.

Sound familiar?

But Isn't Positivity Always a Good Thing?

You've probably experienced hundreds of interactions like this. You might be wondering: How can positivity possibly be *toxic*? That's a pretty strong word. Is it really that bad?

Honestly, positivity is such an integral part of our culture that it feels scary to challenge it. As I continue to research and write about positive thinking, I'm constantly worried about coming across as "negative" while discussing this topic. Every time I try to push back against the *good vibes only* culture, there are inevitably those people who are angry, shocked, and confused. Comments and messages flood my in-box: "How could positivity be toxic?! You've officially lost your mind."

I get it. It's a testament to our total devotion to positivity culture. We've been told that it's the key to happiness—and doctors, therapists, and leaders prescribe it regularly. It makes sense that you might question anyone who tells you otherwise. But behind closed doors, my clients, friends, and family have been telling me for years how much they despise the constant pressure to put a positive spin on everything. They're feeling disconnected from their peers who tell them "It'll all be OK" and to "Look on the bright side." They know this isn't working, and they're desperate for another way.

So before we get started, let's clear something up: *positivity isn't all bad.*

When used correctly, it's great. Experts agree that positive feelings like gratitude, contentment, optimism, and self-confidence can lengthen our lives and improve our health. Many of these claims are exaggerated, but there *is* value in positive thinking. People who report having more positive feelings are more likely to have a rich social life, to be more active, and to engage in more health-promoting behaviors. I think we can all agree that it is healthy to feel "positive" when it comes from a genuine place.

But somewhere along the way, we constructed this idea that being a "positive person" means you're a robot who has to see the good in literally *everything*. We force positivity on ourselves because society tells us to, and anything less is a personal failure. Negativity is seen as the enemy, and we chastise ourselves and the people around us when they succumb to it. If you're not positive, you're simply not trying hard enough. If you're not positive, you're a drag to be around.

Healthy positivity means making space for both reality and hope. Toxic positivity denies an emotion and forces us to suppress it. When we use toxic positivity, we are telling ourselves and others that this emotion shouldn't exist, it's wrong, and if we try just a little bit harder, we can eliminate it entirely.

> **Healthy positivity means making space for both reality and hope.**

I know people are tired of positivity being forced on them in moments of struggle, but confronting it and questioning it publicly feels like we are going up against something so massive and pervasive.

Let's do it anyway.

Shame Disguised as Positivity

So you lost your job, and your friend just told you that you shouldn't be upset. The moment the words "At least . . ." left their mouth, the conversation was over. There was no more space for your emotions or your processing. You were being pulled into the land of positivity whether you were ready or not. So you shut down and tried to figure out how the heck you could become more grateful and positive without inconveniencing anyone with your stress, worry, or shame.

This seemingly minor interaction causes you to start suppressing your feelings about the situation, and you act like nothing's wrong. You don't feel great; you're still sad and jobless. But whenever an emotion comes up, you shut it down. You decide to fake it 'til you make it—except it isn't working. Your sleep is getting worse; you don't want to be around people because then you have to be fake, and you're too nervous to ask anyone for advice. Instead of dealing, you plaster positive quotes on your Instagram feed and hope that your mood will turn around.

This is how we enter the shame spiral of toxic positivity. We get mad at ourselves for having a feeling, tell ourselves that we shouldn't be feeling it, and then get mad again when a couple of "just smile" platitudes don't bring us endless positivity. It's a never-ending, soul-sucking spiral, and I want to help you get out of it.

Toxic Positivity Is Denial

As a therapist, I spend my day listening to people talk about their emotions and experiences. This type of work gives me a view of the human experience that you really can't get anywhere else. Most sessions revolve around the word *should*. People feel like they *should* be happier or that something they're doing is preventing them from being happy, so they jump right back into that positivity shame spiral. In these cases, I help people examine the *should*. Where did they learn that? Is it true? Is it based on fact? Can they look at the situation in a different, more nuanced way? Others, like Dave, use positivity to deny that difficult emotions even exist.

Dave sits across from me on a tiny sofa, beaming. He's sharing about how great he feels and his wonderful family. He reports that he's genuinely happy; all he needs to do is try a little bit harder. This conversation would feel normal and quite promising in any other context, except for the fact that Dave and I are meeting in a residential mental health facility where he has been admitted until further notice. He's here because he likes to drink, and some people in his life think it's getting out of control. Dave tells me he likes to drink because he is a happy and social guy. He doesn't see any problem with it and thinks everyone around him is kind of a buzzkill. *Don't all happy and social guys drink this much?*

Dave is always smiling. Watching him bounce around the clinic among the more morose, pensive, and outwardly suffering patients is confusing and maybe even disturbing at times. He loves to use positive thinking as a coping skill and is really proud of his ability to always appear happy. But his drinking, his inability to experience emotions, and his lack of close relationships tell me a completely different story. In actuality, his positive attitude has become a huge issue in our sessions and in his recovery.

Because of his "everything's great!" approach to life, Dave struggles with emotional expression. This isn't as uncommon as you may think. He can't access any feelings that aren't positive and tends to shut down whenever things get too heavy. I can see that he drinks to deal with these feelings, but Dave is having trouble with this connection. Because of this, we really can't process anything from his past or plan for future issues with his mental health. Accepting that his drinking is problematic isn't even on the table. He believes any struggle will work itself out and there's nothing a positive attitude can't fix. Positive thinking has become Dave's shield, and until he learns to put it down, change will be nearly impossible.

My clients who live the most fulfilling lives are those who can experience challenging emotions. They don't just slap on a smile. They work through any shame that comes with the struggle to get to the other side. When we know that our emotions are meant to be experienced and that they're not something we need to run from, it makes it easier to move into a place of optimism because we know that we can handle whatever comes our way.

How Positivity Becomes Toxic

Positivity becomes toxic when used:

- in conversations where someone is looking for support, validation, or compassion and instead is met with a platitude.

- to shame people into feeling like they're not doing enough, working hard enough, or that their difficult emotions are invalid.

- to shame ourselves for not being happy enough or positive enough.

- to deny our reality.

- to gaslight or silence someone who has legitimate concerns or questions.

- to tell people everything bad in their life is their fault.

At its core, toxic positivity is both well-intentioned *and* dismissive. We often use it to:

- end the conversation.

- tell someone why they shouldn't be feeling what they're feeling.

- convince people they can be happy all the time (if they try hard enough).

- always appear positive and carefree.

- deny or avoid our current situation.

- avoid taking responsibility.

- attempt to make people feel better.

Authenticity Matters

I believe that we use platitudes because we want to be helpful. I don't think anyone actually means to hurt someone with positive phrases. That's why the concept of toxic positivity can be so triggering. It makes us wonder: *How can I be toxic when I'm just trying to help?*

Being genuine and authentic in moments of crisis or pain is important. It's how we show up for each other and demonstrate that we're listening and we get it. You're not going to be able to do this for everyone all the time, but you can do it when it matters. When we show up authentically, rather than using toxic positivity, we're validating that what the other person is going through is real, empathizing, and not sugarcoating or denying their experience. You may not totally agree with how they're handling it or their interpretation of the situation, but you're authentically trying to connect and show up for them. You're saying that you hear them by sitting with them and allowing them to show up fully (in a safe way that doesn't violate your boundaries, of course).

Remember the friend who was trying to comfort you when you lost your job? They used toxic positivity when they said, "At least you have all this time off now! It could be so much worse. Think about how much you're going to learn from this." Of course they weren't trying to hurt you. The language of positivity isn't something we just make up on the spot. It's ingrained in us. We've been conditioned to repeat these phrases over and over and have heard other people using them since we were kids. We believe positivity will eventually work (even if we think it's not helping us). It's almost as if we're afraid to admit it's not working because we have been told so many times that it should. Your friend isn't toxic or a bad person; they're just repeating what they've been told to say by countless self-help books, social media affirmations, friends, and family members.

The thing is, regardless of intention, language matters. It impacts how we see ourselves and the world. The words we choose change our brains and profoundly impact how we relate to others. If we want to communicate effectively and make other people feel supported, we must first understand the world they live in. When we use toxic positivity, we're more focused on saying the thing we've been told to say than genuinely listening to, connecting with, and learning about the person in distress.

Most positivity lingo lacks nuance, compassion, and curiosity. It comes in the form of blanket statements that tell someone *how to feel* and that *the feeling they're currently having is wrong*. These two things are immediate clues that positivity isn't inherently helpful. If you genuinely want to help someone, I'm sure you don't want them to feel bad. Platitudes like this can become especially toxic when someone is sharing something vulnerable, talking about their emotions, or trying to explain a hardship or struggle.

When it comes to using positive language or positivity, the impact depends on your timing, your audience, and the topic being discussed.

Timing

We often rush into positivity because we genuinely want people to feel better. We hope that if we say just the right thing, their pain will go away. We also selfishly hope it works so we can move away from a difficult topic and save ourselves the pain of being with someone who is struggling. I think we can all admit that sitting with someone who is crying, distressed, or upset can be hard. You just want to make it all better.

Unfortunately, moving too quickly can lead to disappointment on all fronts. It may cause the person we're comforting to feel silenced and ashamed, and it often leaves us feeling ineffective and disconnected.

Timing is everything. Before encouraging someone to look on the bright side, it's important to remember:

- Time doesn't heal all wounds. People process things at different speeds, and they get to decide where they are in their healing process.

- When experiencing distress, everyone reacts differently. Unless their reaction is life-threatening or directly harmful to you or someone who needs protection (like a child or the elderly), it's OK to let someone experience their feelings. You don't have to fix it.

- People often need to accept the reality of a situation before moving forward.

- Not all situations have a silver lining or a positive spin. Some things are just really, really hard, and that's OK.

- Watching people in pain is very difficult. Have compassion for yourself, too.

Try to avoid using a positive platitude:

- When someone is crying about something or clearly in the midst of experiencing a difficult emotion.

- Immediately after an event happens (like right after someone gets fired from their job).

- While at a funeral or when someone is dying.

- When someone tells you that they just want you to listen.

- When someone tells you they don't want advice.

- While a distressing event is literally happening.

- When you don't have a complete understanding of what is going on.

Your Audience

Regardless of our intent, we don't get to decide the impact of our words. The person on the receiving end of your support gets to determine if your positive platitudes are helpful or unhelpful. This is why considering your audience is so important.

Whenever I ask my community to share their experiences with toxic positivity, many responses include God or religion. Examples like "They're with God now" or "It was all part of God's plan" flood my in-box. This is a perfect example of why considering our audience matters. Religion, faith, and God can be extremely supportive for some people and not at all for others. When we use our values or religion to support someone else, we're not considering our audience. Instead, we're taking what is helpful for *us* and assuming it will be supportive for them.

This is also true when we're speaking to someone who struggles with depression. Most depressed people want to be happy. They know how hard it is to get there and are consistently reminded of how challenging it is to reach that goal. When we tell someone who is depressed to "just be happy," we aren't considering our audience. We're trivializing their daily battle and making it seem simple. If they could "just be happy," wouldn't they have done it by now? If it were that simple, we wouldn't have such high rates of depression in this country.

The person you are supporting gets to decide how they would like to be supported and you get to decide if you're willing and able to provide that support. We have to consider what we know about their current situation or struggle and be sensitive to that.

Here are some things to take into consideration:

- Has this person told me how they like to be supported?

- Have I asked them how they like to be supported?

- Do they usually react well when I use positive platitudes? Do they say "Thank you" or tell me I was helpful? Do they seem to feel better?

- Does the conversation seem to end whenever I use one of these platitudes or try to encourage someone to be more positive?

It's important to know your audience and how they like to be helped. When in doubt, ask! This will allow you to be the best support person possible.

Difficult Topics

Certain topics are really distressing and heavy for many people. My research and client work reveal that toxic positivity and platitudes are particularly unhelpful—even harmful—for the following topics and situations:

- Infertility and pregnancy loss

- Grief and loss

- Illness and disability

- Romantic relationships, breakups, or divorce

- Family and family estrangement

- Career trouble or job loss

- Physical appearance

- After a traumatic event

- Pregnancy and parenting

- Racism, sexism, transphobia, homophobia, ableism, sizeism, classism, or other types of prejudice

- Mental health issues

These are hard topics. They're really personal and layered. Talking about any of these topics is not the same as complaining about waiting in a long line or saying that your feet hurt. These are issues that shake us to our core and expose our vulnerability. We have to handle them with a different type of sensitivity, both within ourselves and for others. This is where true emotional processing is crucial and must be encouraged. If you feel tempted to reach for a platitude when learning of these troubles or facing them yourself, pause. Tune in to the deeper emotions of the moment and try to respond from a place of acceptance and support.

How Too Much Positivity Harms Us

Positive thinking is often a Band-Aid on a bullet wound. Instead of helping, it leads to emotional suppression, which is destructive to our bodies, minds, relationships, and society. The evidence clearly indicates that emotional suppression is ineffective, taxing, and maladaptive. It leads to a worsened mood, negative feelings about social interactions, continued negative emotions, and even diminished positive emotions. Emotional suppression also has significant consequences for our physical health. It doesn't matter what type of emotion you're suppressing, positive or negative—the act of suppression leads to physical stress on the body. It has been shown to impact blood pressure and memory and increases the risk for diabetes and heart disease.

In a broader sense, a "good vibes only" culture is toxic for our relationships and society. When we reinforce that some emotions are "bad," we miss out on the closeness that develops through vulnerability. Sadly, positivity is often used as a weapon to diminish the experience of certain groups. When we say things like "Can't we all just love each other?" in response to discrimination, we invalidate the real experiences marginalized people endure every day. Toxic positivity in these situations places all the responsibility on the individual instead of on the systems and institutions that make positive thinking an impossible solution.

Common Examples of Toxic Positivity and Why They Hurt

People have sent me thousands of messages about the sayings that invalidate them when they're struggling. Now that we know it's all about timing, our audience, and the topic, let's break down some typical examples of toxic positivity and why they're particularly unhelpful in a variety of situations. Later in this book, we will talk about what you might choose to do or say instead.

"Life will never give you more than you can handle."
Bad things don't happen to people because they can handle it. Some people aren't strong enough in that moment to handle what has been thrown at them and that's OK. When we say this, we're implying that there's always a lesson in every challenge, that people are chosen for specific challenges, and that they better rise to the occasion.

"You'll be fine."
Telling someone who is in a state of panic or shock that they will be fine isn't convincing or comforting. It typically isn't based on fact (How do you know? What does "fine" mean, anyway? Isn't it pretty subjective?) and quickly shuts down the conversation.

"Don't cry!"
We usually say this because we're uncomfortable sitting with someone who is emotional. Crying is helpful, normal, and allowed. Telling someone not to cry implies that what they're doing is wrong and encourages them to suppress their emotions.

"Just smile!"
Telling someone to smile when they're upset is painful. Forcing anyone to be happy in a moment of struggle is oppression.

"You have so much to be grateful for."
We can feel upset while also being grateful for what we have, but this feels dismissive and silencing in a moment of struggle.

"Time heals all wounds."
Time doesn't heal all wounds. Telling someone this when they are very much not over something can be insensitive and shaming. Only they get to decide when they've healed, and sometimes we don't "get over it."

"Just be happy/positive!"

If it were that easy, we would all be doing it. This simplifies a very challenging and complex emotional process, especially when facing serious mental health challenges.

"At least it's not _____."

Anything with "at least" in front of it is minimizing. It's not helpful to compare suffering. (At least you're not dead, right? Is that helpful? Didn't think so.)

"Your attitude is everything."

This is an oversimplification of our reality. Many studies show that an entire network of factors contributes to someone's success. Their attitude is an important factor, but it is *not* everything.

"Be grateful for what you learned."

This is particularly harmful after someone has experienced a traumatic event. Sadly, I commonly see this used after someone has been abused. Yes, we will eventually learn from our struggles, but it doesn't mean we have to be grateful for that lesson. Often the price is too high.

"It could be worse."

True. It could also be better. This statement minimizes and also informs the person that their suffering isn't justified because it's not the "worst."

"Cut all negativity out of your life."
A life without negativity is a life devoid of learning and growth. If we cut all negative people or experiences out of our life, we will end up alone and emotionally stunted.

"Never give up."
There are certain situations when giving up is very brave or necessary. It doesn't always mean that the person was weak or couldn't handle it. Often it means they were strong enough to know when to walk away.

"Everything happens for a reason."
This is quite harmful following a traumatic event or a loss. Some things do not happen for a reason, or the reason is not apparent. Telling someone they were attacked, lost a child, or suffered an illness for a "reason" can be extremely confusing and dismissive.

None of these statements give us the opportunity to share or get to a deeper level about what's going on. None of them make room for emotional expression or connection. They're nice—and they're empty.

The Rise of Positive Thinking

Positive thinking being sold as a cure isn't a new phenomenon. Today we have *good vibes only* bumper stickers and self-help gurus telling you to just be happy, but we've been drinking the Kool-Aid for centuries.

The positive thinking we see today in the West has largely been a haphazard adaptation and combination of numerous wellness traditions from other parts of the world. It all started when a group of white men arrived in the "New World," formally known today as the United States of America. Now we know this world wasn't exactly "new"; a lot of people were already living here.

Most of the men who arrived in the New World were Calvinists. They believed that all men were evil at their core and that God was the only one who could save them from their sins. Who would be saved was already predetermined, so there wasn't much you could do about that. Idleness or pleasure was considered a sin. You were expected to work constantly and hope you were among one of the chosen. It wasn't exactly a fun time to be alive, and Calvinism wasn't sending out the inspiring message the "New World" wanted.

With Calvinism as the prevailing religious belief and social influence, the settlers had a serious branding problem and they knew it. They found exactly what they needed in the New Thought movement. The New Thought movement was adopted as a way to give people hope and improve morale. It was much more uplifting and completely ignored the reality of their current circumstances. Believers proposed that if humans could access the unlimited power of Spirit, they would have control over the spiritual world. This idea was enticing because it gave people more power and control over their lives than they possessed under Calvinism. The groundwork was being laid for a more positive, upbeat New World, where the pursuit of happiness was both expected and mandatory. Unfortunately, nothing about the world had changed yet, except for this new outlook.

Phineas Parkhurst Quimby, the father of New Thought, really took positive thinking to the next level in the 1800s. Quimby believed that all illness originated in the mind and was caused by mistaken beliefs. If someone could become one with their "mind" and leverage the power of the universe, they could cure themselves. It was way easier to disseminate a new scientific idea in the 1800s and the theory was never subjected to rigorous scientific testing. But this belief persists today in many of the Law of Attraction texts and within various alternative healing communities. Mary Baker Eddy, one of Quimby's patients, continued to promote the idea that the cause of disease was rooted in the human mind. She proposed that illness or want did not exist and were simply "temporary delusions." Quimby used this theory to explain why bad things happen in the world and to reinforce why negativity must be avoided.

Positive thinking continued in the nineteenth century with the mind-cure movement and emphasized the healing power of positive emotions and beliefs. William James, the first American psychologist, became a fervent defender and believer in the mind-cure movement and New Thought. He didn't fully understand how mind-cure worked, but he was impressed with this innovative way of thinking and seeing the world. He had his criticisms, though, and was actually the first person to recognize toxic positivity. While he agreed that New Thought was helping to counteract the depressive nature of Calvinism and paving the way for a more positive way of thinking and living, he was aware that this new religion completely sidestepped the reality of tragedy. James pointed out that it was only suitable for "healthy-minded people" and simply offered a temporary solution. He also recognized how cruel it was to tell the depressed and oppressed to just smile and ignore the systems that oppress them. James was signaling that we were headed toward a culture of toxic positivity, but no one was listening. All people heard was that there was a possibility they could control the universe and get everything they ever wanted, simply by changing their thoughts. Most people couldn't resist that possibility; they still can't.

As New Thought spread, it infiltrated the medical community and was used to treat physical ailments. Obviously, this didn't work for the more infectious diseases, but people continued to believe that if an illness could not be cured, it was not "real" and was simply a bid for attention or an attempt to get out of chores or social obligations. Keep in mind, at the time, women were believed to be doomed to invalidism and the treatment of choice for most ailments was lying in a dark room for weeks. The idea that we can fight certain diseases by being more positive persists to this day.

In the wake of the New Thought movement, significant scientific and medical advancements started happening and the germ theory of disease gained traction. This forced the New Thought believers to shift their focus away from health and wellness to wealth and success. The American obsession with power began to grow as they dominated new territories and groups of people, all in the name of wealth and prosperity. *Think and Grow Rich* by Napoleon Hill quickly became the positive thinking bible of the 1930s. Hill proposed a formula and rules that, if followed exactly, would lead the reader to a "white heat of desire for money." The formula is apparently not supposed to be hard work, but if it isn't done correctly, "You will fail!" This is when we start to see the beginning of a cultural fixation on both power and positivity. This obsession is still a regular feature in the workplace today.

Positive thinking was now officially becoming the doctrine of the young nation. Instead of Calvinism's focus on monitoring your thoughts and feelings for signs of sin, laziness, or self-indulgence, positive thinking encourages monitoring your thoughts for "negativity." In 1952, Norman Vincent Peale introduced *The Power of Positive Thinking*, further solidifying the relationship between religion and positivity. The book was a publishing phenomenon and remained on the *New York Times* bestseller list for 186 weeks. It became the first modern how-to guide for those who wanted to transform their lives and would become the foundation for thousands of self-help books and for gurus to launch their careers.

Eugenics was also extremely popular in the early 1900s thanks to Charles Darwin. According to Darwin's theory, emotional expression and emotional self-control are the key markers of evolutionary differences between the "higher" and "lower" developed species. Evolutionary superiority was epitomized by happiness, optimism, and self-control. Darwin believed that negative emotions associated with mental illness were signs of weakness and proposed methods for getting rid of people who have high levels of depression or anger. His survival-of-the-fittest logic meant that anyone who expressed negative emotions or had little emotional control would detract from the happiness of others. These theories were used to maintain the prevailing social order and resulted in the death, isolation, and condemnation of many, including the physically and mentally disabled or ill, queer and transgender individuals, and other marginalized communities. People who subscribed to Darwin's theories about emotional health believed that if they could eliminate anything or anyone that might lead to a negative outcome, prosperity and happiness would be ensured.

The field of psychology also began to shift toward the pursuit of happiness. Two leading psychologists, John B. Watson and G. Stanley Hall, proposed a universal utopian vision where people would be happy and productive all the time. There was a war on negative emotional states and the people who both experience and induce them. In his key textbook *Psychology: From the Standard of a Behaviorist*, Watson states that psychology's main concern was to "engineer healthy individuals who were not feebleminded and lacked anger, fear, and attachments." The prevailing belief was that people could think themselves out of emotional states and ultimately control their destiny through their thoughts. If one could not do this, they were simply weak and needed to be separated from the strong.

Today, we have a multibillion-dollar positive-thinking industry with conferences, books, support groups, motivational speakers, and more. Positive thinking has become the bedrock of the self-help industry and is routinely encouraged and celebrated by people across the globe. Self-help gurus, therapists, and coaches continue to tell us that we're only one positive thought away from a better life, and there are more than ten thousand books about positive thinking on the market today. International bestsellers like *The Secret* and *The Law of Attraction* have become synonymous with positive thinking, abundance, wealth, and success. They propose that you can use the power of positive thinking in every aspect of your life—including your finances, health, relationships, and career. Not unlike Calvinism, the positive thinking movement encourages us to monitor our thoughts for negativity relentlessly and always remain vigilant. Books, worksheets, mantras, and constant self-evaluation are always the weapons of choice in the fight against the real enemy, negativity.

Thanks to widely published literature and professional endorsements, the push for positive thinking has infiltrated all areas of our lives. We're expected to be happy at work, at home, in our relationships, and in the face of tragedy. The body positivity movement wants us to be positive about our bodies. People ask, "Why can't we just get along?" and tell us to "Just love each other" in the face of rampant discrimination and inequality. A positive attitude has become the prescription of choice for anyone fighting disease or living with a disability. Classrooms, hospitals, and workplaces are littered with posters urging us to find meaning and happiness in just about everything. The modern office is filled with Ping-Pong tables and bright sofas—almost seeming to demand "You will have fun here!" We scroll through endless positive quotes, smiling faces, and upbeat social media captions. Gurus and motivational speakers blame our lack of progress on our negative thinking.

The pressure to be happy and look happy has never been greater. We must find a silver lining, a positive spin, a good reason. Cut all negative people out of your life; they're bringing you down. Smile more. Good vibes only. Live, laugh, love. I'm sending you light and love. #Grateful in some weird cursive font. It never ends. We're told time and time again that we can't achieve anything without thinking positively. There is nothing it cannot fix. It's an obligation we must fulfill.

> **The pressure to be happy and look happy has never been greater.**

But if the key to a full life is positive thinking, then why are so many of us still miserable?

Why Positivity Is So Enticing and Attractive

Tory enters my office one afternoon. She's well-dressed and I can tell she invests a lot of time in her appearance. She seems nervous as she fidgets on my sofa. Tory shares a long history of self-improvement with me. We talk about retreats, supplements, healers, dietitians, life coaches, all her previous therapists, and how she devours self-help books on the weekends. She tells me that she starts her day with a gratitude list and ends it with a positive quote. I learn that her mirror is littered with Post-it notes that say "You're amazing!" and "You got this!" She gazes at the floor and admits that what she's doing clearly isn't working. It's obvious that there's an immense sense of guilt around this and she's hesitant to share it with me. She thinks it *should* work and when it doesn't, it means she's a failure. She believes that she must just be doing it wrong.

Tory's therapeutic goal is "happiness," but I'm not sure either one of us knows what that looks like yet. Every week she tells me about something new that she's trying; this will be the thing that makes her happy. She can't seem to get off the self-improvement merry-go-round.

We discover that what she actually wants is to feel happy all the time. She doesn't want to struggle, she wants to appear positive, and she wants to be loved. According to Tory, negative people are annoying and unlovable. Positive people are the best type of people and that's what she aspires to be. Tory is burned out from the constant pursuit of happiness and it's obvious she's been searching for the answer to this problem for quite some time. She's done everything she's "supposed" to do according to all the self-help gurus and motivational speakers out there. I understand her frustration and try to level with her: "What would happen if you weren't happy all the time? Would that be OK?" Tory looks back at me with a blank stare and I can tell she has no idea how to answer these questions.

Self-acceptance is part of her problem. She can't accept that she already has everything she needs inside her to be whole. She's struggling with the reality that the world is determined to always make her feel like she's missing something so that they can sell her a product or get her to change. Tory has been sold the lie that there is this oasis of positivity and happiness on the other side of her self-improvement journey. She can't let go of her constant need to fix and improve because it makes her feel in control. She refuses to look at the role her cold and rejecting spouse has played in her life or how stressful her job is, because she should be able to just control her thoughts and emotions in the face of anything. Until Tory learns to look within herself and consider the impact the world has on her, she'll continue to search for control in the wrong places and blame herself when she falls short.

Positive Thinking Gives Us the Illusion of Hope and Control

I can relate to Tory because I've been her. I know the feeling of searching for relief all too well. It's the constant quest for that one thing that's going to make you happy—a better body, more friends, a bigger house, the list goes on. It's exhausting, and there's something so enticing about this search. It's filled with possibility, the potential for control, and a desire to be loved. It seems impossible that self-help and the quest for positivity could ever hurt us. We're convinced that we just have to try a little harder and we'll finally get there.

Positive thinking is so attractive for a few key reasons:

- It makes us feel like we have control over our life.

- It allows us to absolve our responsibility for other people's lives.

- There's always something concrete to blame when something goes wrong—your thoughts.

Most positive thinking literature provides us with a simple formula: change your thoughts, change your life. This is so powerful because it taps into our biggest fear as humans: uncertainty. When we know, we feel safe, and safety is everything. People have been searching for the answer to "Why do bad things happen?" and "How can I get everything I want?" since the beginning of time. We will probably never stop searching for those answers.

People who practice the Law of Attraction, or other types of positive thinking and manifesting, propose that they've cracked the code to the universe. They know exactly what we need to do, step by step, to get what we want. No questions asked. If we don't get what we want, it's because we didn't do it correctly or didn't try hard enough. These are the only factors involved in the equation. This means, with the right attitude and an abundance of positivity, we will have control over our lives, everyone will be responsible for themselves, and we will always know who and what to blame when things go wrong. It gives us a framework to understand everything in the universe, including illness, discrimination, war, natural disasters, job loss, death, and more.

Sounds pretty incredible, right? Sounds a little too good to be true to me.

Start Them Young

Most parents or caregivers say, "I just want a happy kid," and who doesn't want that? A "happy" child to most parents signifies a job well done. It seems like such a simple goal to have for our children. Instead, we start feeling the pressure to be happy and positive from the moment we step into the world.

A recent study is entitled "Happier Babies Have an Edge." I feel my stomach twist as I read this headline. Wow, now even the babies need to be happy if they want to get ahead! But it makes sense. Think about how we talk about babies. So many adults will say, "They were such a happy baby!" or "Gosh, they never stopped crying as a baby." Infants are categorized as positive or negative, easy baby or hard baby. Everyone obviously wants a happy baby! They're easier to care for, and they demand much less from us than colicky, screaming babies. They also tend to receive more praise and more positive attention from parents because a happier baby will likely lead to a more well-rested, happier caregiver. Your temperament as a child is being watched and it becomes part of your story. It's probably something your family still talks about today.

This particular study found that happiness during infancy predicted childhood IQ and adult educational success. The researchers looked at how often children experience positive and negative emotions and the role that plays in their growth. We know positive emotions like joy or love increase creativity, problem-solving, and kindness. So the more children experience positive emotions, the more time they will spend playing, learning, and socializing. This directly contributes to their development. Children experiencing more negative emotions, like sadness or anger, will have fewer opportunities to learn because they are focused on getting rid of or avoiding whatever is bothering them. Makes sense, but the researcher carefully points out that this was a very low-risk research pool. Children raised in more adverse conditions are more likely to experience fewer positive emotions and more negative emotions that could reduce happiness because of their environment. Other studies have also found that high adversity is linked to lower IQs, poorer academic performance, and decreased happiness. So one could argue that it's not the happiness that contributes to the child's growth, but their ability to be raised in a loving, supportive environment with minimal adversity that leads to more happiness and, in turn, more opportunities for growth, development, and happiness.

As young children develop, their emotional experiences literally become part of the fiber of their brains. This critical stage of development has enormous implications. The Australian Temperament Project, a longitudinal study conducted by psychologists for more than thirty years, looked at how temperament develops and why some babies are happier than others. They found that temperament is relatively stable over time, with very few children experiencing radical change. But temperament *can* be modified through positive experiences like bonding with caregivers and growing up in a stable environment. Some babies are just born happier than others, and some may become more positive due to more supportive environments and experiences. But from a young age, children know that happiness and positivity are certainly rewarded.

Young children quickly begin assessing how their caregivers manage their own moods and how those moods predict their behavior. They become skilled at assessing the emotional landscape of their home, their caregivers, and the other people they spend time with. This is a tool for survival. They learn what seems to upset their caregivers and if their report of their mood lines up with their behavior. Because the emotional health of young children is directly tied to the emotional and social characteristics of the environment where they are raised, caregivers have immense influence. In many homes where certain emotions are discouraged or shamed, positivity often becomes the default and encouraged emotional response.

If you grew up in a home where emotional expression was discouraged, this might have happened:

- Caregivers said things were "fine" even when they weren't.

- Caregivers told you not to cry when you were upset or to "man up" and "act tough."

- You were told that discussing any type of concern or complaint was "negativity."

- Your caregivers rarely showed challenging or difficult emotions and if they did, they denied them or tried to cover them up.

- Caregivers' reports of their emotions didn't match their behavior (e.g., they're crying and saying everything is great).

- Caregivers didn't discuss emotions openly with you.

- Emotions were categorized as "good" or "bad."

- It was challenging for you to read your caregiver's emotions.

- You spent a lot of time and energy trying to assess the emotions of the family unit.

- You were not taught how to label your emotions effectively.

As children, we might hear statements like "Positive people are the best people!" and "No one likes a Negative Nancy!" These statements become beliefs and those beliefs impact our behaviors. When an adult models that positivity should always be the mood of choice, children learn through observation that even when things are bad, we should try to make the best of it. No matter what. As a result, many of us haven't learned how to tune in to how we actually feel or why it matters.

This reinforcement continues throughout our lifetime, especially at school. Walk into any school and you'll see that the walls are covered with posters that exclaim "Be happy!" and "You look best with a smile!" Schools and teachers insist that learning is supposed to be fun and you should just enjoy it. Academic institutions spend large amounts of money to keep children "happy" and improve morale but continue to struggle to provide adequate resources like mental healthcare and updated learning materials.

As we age, the modern workplace becomes the place where positivity culture entraps us. There are parties, awards, and meetings dedicated solely to employee happiness. You're encouraged to have a good attitude at all times, be grateful, love your work, and leave the rest at home. Employees who offer constructive criticism or feedback are often considered "negative," and a positive attitude is deemed essential if you want a raise or a promotion.

Having a positive attitude is also routinely celebrated and rewarded in society. Think about the people who are celebrated in the media. We hear tons of stories about:

- People who have made the best out of "so little."

- "Inspiration porn" about people who are living with illness or disability but seem to smile through it all.

- A "model minority" member, in an attempt to erase the negative image of racism, sexism, classism, or other prejudice.

Our obsession with positivity is all around us. Struggles are now classified as "opportunities." Triggers are "teachers." Grief is now "love with nowhere to go." Weaknesses are actually "emerging strengths." We came to believe that positivity was the key to happiness, wellness, and longevity. Our intentions were good, but somehow we got lost along the way.

Can You Really Manifest Anything?

Manifestation is one of the main tools used by positivity enthusiasts. According to the Law of Attraction, manifestation is defined as "something that is put into your physical reality through thought, feelings, and beliefs." It can be done through meditation, visualization, or using your conscious and subconscious. People who practice manifestation propose that if you are constantly feeling negative emotions, you will attract negativity. This means that you attract exactly what is meant for you. If you are positive and visualize what you want, it will come to you. People are encouraged to focus on what they want, eliminate all toxic people that will get in the way, and to be very patient. While you wait for it to manifest, you can continue living life normally, and there isn't anything specific you need to do to make it happen.

Sounds easy, right?

This advice is in direct conflict with most psychological research about motivation and goal achievement. There's no planning for obstacles that may occur, no assessment of individual abilities, and no action plan. It also implies that bad things typically only happen to people who want, envision, and manifest bad things. These people are vibrating at a "low frequency" and pumping out bad vibes into the world. But certainly we have evidence that this isn't true. Bad things happen to good people every single day.

The problem arises when we don't take into consideration our own limitations, systemic influences, challenges that may arise, and an appropriate action plan. It's very easy to follow this simple manifestation scheme and blame the individual if they can't make it happen. Didn't get that new car you want? You must've been too negative. Try again!

Manifestation does have some essential ingredients that are not toxic or detrimental. In order to get what we want, we have to know what that thing is and visualize it. We have to believe that achieving it is possible. There has to be a delicate interplay between individual and community responsibility. We can integrate external factors that may impede certain goals while also encouraging and inspiring people to take the reins and make their life exactly what they want. As an alternative to traditional manifestation, I really like using Dr. Gabriele Oettingen's WOOP tool to help you choose, achieve, and evaluate your goals. Start with these questions:

1. What is your Wish?

2. What is the ideal Outcome?

3. What Obstacles might you come across?

4. What is your Plan to achieve this?

You can use WOOP to achieve pretty much anything. It will also help you identify solid goals and where to begin.

Recognizing self-imposed or imagined limits is important because we can work to push past them. Recognizing the limits that are truly part of your life doesn't mean giving up. It's orienting yourself toward what is right for you.

But I Don't Want to Be Negative

When people hear the term *toxic positivity*, they often think that I'm implying that we should be negative all the time. That's not helpful, either, and it's totally not what this is about. It's about balance. Being human means making space for the positive, the negative, and everything in between.

We have been bombarded with messages that we need to be happy all the time. When we internalize those beliefs, we put that pressure on ourselves and others. It feels like if we're not able to achieve this mindset, we must be doing something wrong, something must be wrong with us, or we're doing others a huge disservice.

The next few chapters will show you the power of compassion, vulnerability, and curiosity and how they can help us move into a place where we feel seen, supported, connected, and heard. When we have all those needs met, anything is possible.

Reflection

Take a moment to think about your life and answer these questions.

- When did you learn that being positive was important?

- Did your parents encourage you to feel and express different emotions? Did they express a variety of emotions like happiness, anger, sadness, or disappointment?

- Are you worried about appearing "negative"?

- What do you think makes a person truly happy?

WHAT YOU PUT OUT INTO THE WORLD IS EXACTLY WHAT YOU GET BACK.

The world can be cruel and random. Unfortunately, we can put out tons of positive energy and still struggle. Strive for a life that honors your values and has meaning. Do the best you can and know that not everything bad that comes your way is because you attracted it.

Chapter Two

Why Positivity Doesn't Always Work

Toxic positivity has infiltrated a few key areas of our world. From cancer patients to the unemployed to people looking for solace in religion, we've all been sold the story that positive thoughts will make everything better. Today, it's impossible to navigate business, healthcare, religion, or science without being pressured to look on the bright side. There's a reason why this not-so-magic cure is failing us, and it's not your fault.

You're Not Unemployed; You're Funemployed!

Alissa works at a massive law firm. We've been working together since she started as a new associate. Her days and nights are spent hunched over a desk reading lengthy documents. Alissa is miserable, stressed out, overworked, and can't seem to get off the hamster wheel. She tells me about how lucky she is to have this job (a job that, in my opinion, seems to treat her poorly). There are the stories of sexual harassment, the lack of sufficient support, and the late-night calls and emails.

Every month Alissa gets slammed with work, and she's really good at her job, so they give her even more to do. The flood of work is peppered with the occasional mandatory staff meeting, where her boss demands smiles and excitement. Sometimes they play games or wear funny hats to dial up the positive vibes in the office. She tells me about how her boss is visibly annoyed when morale isn't high enough for his liking. From her private conversations, Alissa knows that everyone is burned out and overwhelmed, but no one says a thing in public. They don't speak up because the pay is good, the office is glamorous, and because at the holiday party everyone brags about how great the culture is. To complain would mean you "couldn't handle it" or that you "didn't appreciate what you have."

I can tell from our weekly conversations that Alissa won't last much longer in this environment. She looks drained and gazes out the window as she explains her extreme levels of exhaustion. She knows it's bad, but she just can't break free. We spend weeks working on boundaries and gathering the courage to discuss the issues with her employer. Alissa bravely shares with her boss how she's not sleeping and won't be able to sustain this level of work for much longer. She explains how much she values the job and wants to make it work. In our session, she shares how her boss smirked when she finished. "Be grateful you have the work. People would kill to have this job," he said. She's crying now, and I'm sad for her, but I'm also not surprised.

Despite Alissa's immense bravery, nothing changes at work and we're back in session talking about the exhaustion and the late-night emails and the lack of boundaries again. She's starting to talk herself into staying at the job and "sucking it up," because who leaves a job when there are so many people unemployed and who complains when it's really "not that bad"?

Do Positive People Always Succeed?

According to most business coaches and employers, positivity is a prerequisite for achievement. A quick Google search on "how to be successful" will yield thousands of articles about positive thinking and getting ahead. The most popular business books that promise to help you "get rich," like *Secrets of the Millionaire Mind*, all rely on the power of our mindset. The author, T. Harv Eker, proposes that education, intelligence, skills, timing, work habits, contacts, luck, or choice of job, business, or investment aren't what predicts your financial future. It's all about your mindset and subconscious beliefs. If you want to be rich, you need to be positive. With all these successful programs floating around proposing easy-to-follow formulas, it's a wonder we don't have more millionaires!

The modern workplace has also evolved into a space that demands positivity. Offices are filled with TV screens, video games, bright-colored sofas, and candy. The Google office in Tel Aviv even has an artificial beach and a slide, while one of its London offices features beach huts and meeting rooms shaped like giant dice. Companies are creating office playgrounds and you're expected to have fun. Actually, you *must* enjoy every moment. Heck, you may never want to leave!

You've also probably been told that you need to have a good attitude if you want to get a job or score that next promotion. Instead of being unemployed and lamenting over the loss of employment, money, and opportunity, we're now expected to be "funemployed"! There are entire conferences, books, podcasts, and articles tailored specifically to help unemployed people find the silver lining of job loss. Even losing your job needs to be fun and inspirational! These events often don't integrate outside forces like the job market, the economy, and access to resources. Unemployment is just a mountain that you need to climb with a smile. How lucky are you to have this opportunity! *#Grateful #Funemployed*

Negativity is rarely celebrated in the workplace, and no one wants to receive the ubiquitous title of office "Negative Nancy." Employers expect positivity and even demand it, but is it actually working?

Bring Your Negativity to Work Day

Managing a team isn't easy. Most employers and team leaders would argue that it would be easier if their employees could play nice, smile, and just get their work done. Complaints and negativity do make their jobs much harder. But what they're really striving for here is groupthink. Irving Janis describes this as "the psychological drive for consensus at any cost." It's the perfect description of toxic positivity in the workplace. Groupthink suppresses dissent and the appraisal of alternatives. You're afraid to speak up because it will ruin the vibe, and you really want to be seen as an essential part of the group—a team player. When groupthink is happening, everyone seems to feel comfortable (they actually aren't), and with the right strategies you can avoid tension for a little while. The problem is, it's tough to sustain. Groupthink and the pressure to maintain a facade of positivity makes employees less happy, stifles creativity, and keeps the business stuck.

We really need negativity in the workplace, and it's quite dangerous if we eliminate it, especially in creative industries. Research shows us that toxic positivity stunts creativity and stops you from seeing important pain points that the business or customer may struggle with. Peter Senge, the author of *The Fifth Discipline*, defines creative tension as the ability to articulate the gap between your vision and the problem that needs to be solved. By focusing on the negative, or the problem, you're able to visualize possible solutions. But it's impossible to discover that solution without first really getting to know the problem. This usually involves complaining, venting, lamenting, and purposely pointing out the flaws in something. Most positive thinkers or manifesters would run from this, but it's how we solve some of the world's most significant problems. Without negativity in creative meetings, we wouldn't have that new iPhone update or comfortable tennis shoes. If you encourage a culture where productive disagreement isn't allowed or is discouraged, you'll never come up with solutions.

Positivity also stifles empathy for the customer. If you rush too quickly into positivity, you're unable to understand the customer's pain points. Have you ever gotten the wrong food order at a restaurant? Yes, you want them to replace your meal, but you also want them to show understanding and remorse. If they just walked away and brought you a new plate of food without saying anything, would you be totally satisfied? I know I wouldn't. Genuine empathy requires that we listen, understand, and feel what is happening so that we can create a targeted solution. This means telling the customer you're so sorry for bringing the wrong dish, listening to how frustrating this was for them, agreeing on a solution, following through on the solution, and then checking in to make sure they're satisfied. We can't do any of that without listening to and engaging with negativity.

Many employees report that they're actively discouraged from speaking out about office issues in the name of a "positive work culture" even though federal labor laws explicitly protect employees' right to "complain about working conditions to the public, including customers." Despite these protections, complaints about sexual harassment, lack of diversity, discrimination, and other types of prejudice or critical issues may be silenced in the name of "positivity" or being a "team player." Alissa dealt with this a lot at her job. Everyone was expected to be grateful that it wasn't worse, and nothing ever changed. After she brought up her concerns to her boss and was shut down, she knew she'd never risk complaining again.

Maybe you've experienced this, too. So many people have told me that their complaints are usually met with things like a pizza party, a work happy hour, or more gaslighting like Alissa experienced. This is why so many companies stay stuck. There's a fear that too much "negativity" will ruin the culture. A company cannot move forward without acknowledging the negative. It's the only way to create change and progress.

> *Gaslighting* is the manipulation and control of another person's perspective for unethical reasons over an extended period of time. It's a challenge to your version of reality and forces you to question yourself and your perspective.

How to Avoid Toxic Positivity in the Workplace

There are a few key ways that you can continue to promote a healthy workplace culture while also encouraging creativity, growing your business, and making your employees feel comfortable.

Employee engagement is one of the most important components of a successful workplace. When employees are engaged, they feel valued, secure, supported, and respected. A Gallup poll showed that engagement predicted well-being more than any other type of benefits offered and that employees prefer workplace well-being to material benefits. You can help your team feel engaged in a few simple ways:

- Show genuine interest in your employees' lives by asking questions and demonstrating that you care about more than what they can do for you and the company.

- Show empathy when people are struggling. Brain imaging has shown that when employees recalled a boss that had been unsympathetic, they had increased activation in areas of the brain associated with avoidance and negative emotion. The opposite was true when they remembered an empathic boss.

- Emphasize the meaningfulness and importance of the work. People feel better and do better when they are connected to the mission.

- Treat employees and colleagues with respect, gratitude, trust, and integrity.

- Encourage people to talk about their problems and teach them that the leader has their best interests in mind. Research by Amy Edmondson at Harvard shows that when leaders are inclusive, humble, and encourage their staff to speak up or ask for help, it leads to better learning and performance outcomes.

- Help your employees and colleagues. Jonathan Haidt at New York University discovered that when leaders are fair and self-sacrificing, their employees become more loyal and committed to the company.

- Recognize the differences between negativity and problem-solving. Someone who points out issues in the workplace or proposes new ideas is very different from someone who complains about the coffee flavors.

Creating a healthy workplace is pretty cheap and simple. It doesn't require fancy furniture, a Ping-Pong table, or a bar cart circling the office every afternoon. Be human and show your employees that you care about them. Listen and create a culture of open communication. The results will speak for themselves.

Smile, You Have Cancer

The medical system is where I first became acquainted with toxic positivity. A close family member of mine is chronically ill, disabled, and has been navigating the medical system for years. I also spent my graduate school internship and part of my postgraduate internship working with children and adults who had been diagnosed with a variety of cancers. In my private practice, I now work with adults struggling with chronic illness. At first, I didn't really understand what was going on. I knew I was witnessing something bizarre happening here—from the pink ribbons to the "Get well soon!" banners and a constant focus on positivity in every support group. Honestly, it annoyed me, but I kept drinking the Kool-Aid like everyone else. I naively thought this was just what you had to do to get better. Until I got so annoyed that I began furiously researching positivity and its effectiveness.

As it turns out, I'm not the only one who is annoyed.

The toxic positivity I have witnessed within the healthcare system, from physicians and medical staff, and among the chronic illness community could fill this entire book, but the story I remember most is Alex's story.

Alex was a thirteen-year-old boy with an aggressive type of cancer. I started working with Alex and his mother shortly after his diagnosis. She was a single mother and beyond dedicated to her son and his health. The doctors didn't seem confident that Alex would live much longer. It's tragic when someone is given a prognosis like this one; it's beyond tragic when they're a child. Alex's mother had a habit of wanting to look on the bright side of everything. She refused to use the word *cancer* and constantly referred to the disease as "it." Whenever Alex tried to talk about his illness, his mother would immediately become a Pollyanna. She would tell him to think positive, insist he would beat this, and eventually change the subject to something more cheerful like a TV show or the weather outside. Whenever we would talk about his scans, she followed up every sentence with, "But we're hopeful and we're gonna get through this!" and look at Alex with a pained smile, seemingly begging for reassurance. It was obvious she was in immense pain, cloaked in denial.

As months passed, Alex's prognosis worsened, and his mom's optimism intensified. It became impossible for Alex to discuss his condition with his mother and their relationship was clearly strained because of this. He struggled to put on a brave face at treatment and during hospital stays. The pressure to be happy was getting to him, and he shared that with me in sessions. We processed his grief and discussed his fears. I really wish his mother could have shared those moments with him, and I know she was doing her best to cope with the possibility of losing her child. She was doing what people had told her would work her entire life—thinking positive, manifesting a different outcome, and monitoring her thoughts for any negativity. Meanwhile, Alex was terrified and felt alone.

Alex died and became one of the many people with cancer who try to stay alive and just aren't able to. It wasn't his fault and no amount of positive thinking or manifestation could've changed the outcome. His mother was devastated, as any parent in this situation would be. Honestly, part of me believes that her relentless positivity prevented her from beginning the grieving process with Alex and sharing those last moments with him. She was so focused on making things happy and manifesting a different outcome that she missed out on the person who was right in front of her—her son. It made things so hard for him at the end, too. I know he was terrified and he didn't want her to think he had given up hope. Spending those moments with him wouldn't have changed the trauma of losing a child, but I think it would have lessened the whiplash she felt when she ultimately had to contend with the fact that her positive thoughts didn't match her reality. Now, no amount of positive thinking would take away this pain.

The Miracle Drug

There is a new discourse in healthcare and wellness that seems to argue that if you eat all the right foods, exercise, think positively, meditate, and drink enough water, you will never get ill. Health is routinely described as the absence of illness, and it all begins in the mind. It's a version of wellness that seems to apply only to the privileged and able-bodied, and it places the onus of responsibility completely on the individual. Within this framework, wellness is promised to those who work for it, earn it, and deserve it. This has led to an increased interest in how negative thoughts or emotional pain result in disease.

We know that there is absolutely a relationship between the mind and the body. High levels of stress have been shown to result in diminished immunological response and greater exposure to illness. Positive emotions and positive thinking play an important role in protecting blood pressure and preventing other cardiovascular illnesses. Higher levels of positive emotions are also beneficial for recovery and survival rates in physically diseased patients. There is no doubt that happier people tend to have an easier time remaining healthy or recovering from illness. We also know that having a positive attitude may help someone deal with the challenges of an illness, but the claims that have been made about positive thinking curing illness are extremely exaggerated, or in some cases, completely lacking evidence. Positive thinking is an asset in managing disease, but it is not a cure, nor is negative thinking the cause of all disease.

Toxic positivity is rampant in healthcare. It impacts the treatment that patients pursue, how medical professionals treat their patients, and how we talk about illness collectively. Overly positive people may neglect to buy insurance because they're confident that everything will work out. Individuals who practice the Law of Attraction may avoid physicians or treatments that are honest about their prognosis and consequently more negative, leading to worse health outcomes and possibly even death. Friends and family who don't want to be around "negativity" might be tempted to cut out any friends and family who are struggling with illness because they believe it will bring them down or that it will cause them to become ill, too. Toxic positivity in healthcare leaves us feeling isolated, misunderstood, and ultimately at risk.

There are three key areas where we see toxic positivity in healthcare: among providers, among the patients themselves, and in how the general population speaks about illness. Most healthcare professionals really want to be helpful. But toxic positivity among healthcare providers can lead to unhelpful or even harmful outcomes. It happened with my client Alex. This is the typical pattern: a new physician gets staffed on the case, and likely out of a deep desire to be helpful, they make a lot of promises they probably can't keep. They get really excited about the premise of being the one to make it all better. There are appointments and scans and lab work. The excitement builds over the promise of a breakthrough, but sometimes they just can't make it better. The positive outlook comes crashing down, and the patient is left to pick up the pieces. Many of my clients with chronic health issues report that they purposefully choose not to believe an excited physician in preparation for an inevitable letdown. They simply cannot handle another crash.

Healthcare professionals often prescribe positivity as a treatment for a variety of diagnoses. It may come in the form of a "just be positive and you'll get through this" or "you have nothing to worry about" right before an invasive surgery. The well-intentioned statements are meant to encourage, but they ultimately leave the patient feeling dismissed and misunderstood. Healthcare professionals may also promote toxic positivity and denial simply because it's easier to work with. A positive and optimistic patient generally demands less than a complaining patient. This may inhibit a patient from accepting their reality and falsely believing in an alternate set of facts. Many researchers have argued that the use of toxic positivity in healthcare is unethical and even dangerous. It leads to unfounded assertions of confidence, implies a lack of empathy for the patient, and can cause people to make uninformed decisions about their health.

Toxic positivity has also become pervasive within the chronic illness community. Patients will shame and accuse one another of not trying hard enough and there is a relentless need to appear strong and positive. Social media is filled with stories about patients who cured their illness with positivity; denying or questioning this proposed "treatment" is just negativity. In my work, I've noticed that people with invisible illnesses or disabilities are scared of acting too positive because then people won't believe that they're sick. They're afraid of being too negative because then they aren't being strong or fighting hard enough. They can't win.

The way we talk about illness is also loaded with toxic positivity. With diseases like cancer, you're "fighting" the disease. If you "beat" the illness, you're a hero. If someone "loses" the "battle" with an illness, it's implied that they simply didn't try hard enough. People who use wheelchairs or live with another disability are expected to be inspirational and motivational at all times. There are fundraisers and parades with balloons, ribbons, and prizes where illnesses are spoken about in black-and-white terms—someone has the illness and now they don't. There's little discussion of symptoms, the exorbitant cost of medical treatment, or the isolation and loneliness. We're committed to putting a positive spin on everything. Illness becomes something that we must eradicate with a smile.

The reality is, approximately 133 million Americans are living with incurable and ongoing chronic diseases. An estimated 61 million people in America live with a disability. These are people who may never embody the mainstream definition of health and wellness. They may never "get better." Are all these people just negative? Are they not trying hard enough? Did they manifest this? Absolutely not.

Well-Being > Positive Thinking

The research on the effectiveness of positive thinking as a cure for illness is pretty abysmal. What we do know is that there is a relationship between optimism and better health outcomes. Research shows that optimism is related to a lower mortality rate, better standard of health, a faster recovery rate in some diseases, and an improved immunological response. Yet, we cannot assume that happiness causes good health, because the research has been unable to define the direction in causality. This means that someone who is happier may actually just have a better immune system and rarely get sick, giving them more opportunities for happiness. Or someone who is ill may struggle more with managing their illness, leading to less positive feelings. We simply don't know if the absence of illness makes people happier or if happiness makes people get sick less.

Stress does impact health negatively, and this does not mean that constant positive thoughts, optimism, and affirmations will always lead to good health. Certainly, we all know someone who is extremely positive and has been ill or even died. You probably also know someone who is quite pessimistic, has never eaten a vegetable, and is healthy as can be. Managing stress and improving happiness does not guarantee health because health is influenced by various factors and cannot be reduced to a simple formula.

Positive thinking is a strategy that can help someone overcome unpleasant, unwanted, destructive attitudes and states of mind. It is one way to boost well-being, but many other needs must be met before this strategy becomes effective.

If we want to eradicate toxic positivity from the healthcare system, we have to move away from positivity and instead focus on an expanded definition of *well-being*. Well-being is a metric that shows us when people perceive their lives as going well. Well-being is associated with self-perceived health, healthy behaviors, longevity, social connectedness, productivity, better immune functioning, faster recovery, and decreased risk of disease, illness, and injury. Well-being research also clearly shows us that health is not just the absence of disease; it's way more than that.

We can achieve well-being when certain conditions are met and people are given the space and resources to find meaning in their life, meet their needs, and cope with their environment. Good living conditions, housing, and employment are fundamental to well-being. Instead of focusing on positive thinking as a cure for illness, we would benefit from providing access to a livable wage, housing, safe communities, meaningful relationships, food security, and healthcare. Then, we can focus on improving our thinking. Health doesn't begin and end in the

Health doesn't begin and end in the mind.

mind. It exists within our communities and truly flourishes when people feel empowered and equipped to achieve their unique version of health.

The Rise of a "Good Vibes Only" God

Toxic positivity and religion have a long history. In chapter one, we got to know the Calvinists and their pessimistic tendencies. Most religions were like this at the time. You were inherently sinful and needed to be saved. There was a lot of fire and brimstone; the fear was real. Religion's image overhaul has led to the rise of the "Good Vibes Only" God. This God wants you to be happy and rich. He believes that love fixes everything, and through him, anything is possible. In this church, doubts and anxieties are a sign of lost faith, and anything can be prayed away, even mental illness. Oh, and the Good Vibes Only God believes that everything happens for a reason.

Liz had never been to therapy before. She was a college student at the local university who decided to contact a therapist after years of not sleeping, racing thoughts, and trouble focusing at school. Liz ended up on my couch one Tuesday afternoon, fidgeting with her key chain. "I'm so nervous. My parents would kill me if they knew I was here." I tried to make things more comfortable by asking her some basic questions. Liz finally settled into the couch, and I prompted her, "So why do you think your parents would be mad that you're here?" She paused. "They think I'm exaggerating and that

I've just lost my faith in the church. They want me to pray more and get more involved with our congregation. My mom's always like, 'Liz, God will never give you more than you can handle' . . . but I'm drowning. I can't handle it."

Liz felt guilty that her faith couldn't get her through this. She didn't understand why she was struggling. I had a suspicion there was probably something else she wasn't telling me and it was impacting her faith. We spent weeks talking about God and her relationship with her religion. We talked about church and Bible study and faith. Liz shared so many positive things about her faith, like the hope it gave her during hard times and how the community made her feel at home. One afternoon, Liz shared with me that she thought she might be gay. "I just know I'm doing something wrong. Maybe I'm not trying hard enough. I can't get this feeling to go away."

Liz was struggling with what we would refer to as generalized anxiety disorder and she was terrified of exploring her identity. She met all the criteria and her symptoms were significantly impacting multiple areas of her life. Prayer and faith would likely help her cope, but we both knew they weren't going to "fix" this. Liz also began to accept that if she was gay, prayer wasn't going to change that, either. She also shared that she didn't want to change that.

We continued working together and she eventually worked up the courage to tell her parents that she was in therapy. She was still trying to figure out a way to tell them about everything else. Liz retained her faith in God throughout our work and kept going to church, and she was even praying more. But she was also using other tools like therapy, medication when needed, and coping skills from her Acceptance and Commitment Therapy workbook. Her prayers had changed, too. She wasn't praying that she would change or that someone would fix her. Instead, she was praying for acceptance, love, and strength. Liz had found a way to integrate her faith into her life in a way that made sense for her—and that started with accepting that she is exactly the way that she needs to be.

God Wants You to Be Happy

Religion and spirituality have always influenced our mental health and have long been a part of the cultural landscape. Religion began as a more omnipresent and scary force, with its language of sin, death, and hell. Various religions have commonly used fear, social shame, and the promise of hope to encourage people to live better lives and play by the rules. Unfortunately, this type of religious doctrine eventually takes a toll on people; we saw this with Calvinism.

Research shows that social shame only hurts and is a counterproductive way of bonding people. People eventually started to grow weary of the traditional, fear-based teachings that were common across religious sects. Modern religious figures recognized that the old ways of promoting religion were no longer working. They needed to find new ways to bring people together and get them excited about religion and that, my friends, is how the Good Vibes Only God was born.

Today, many popular preachers are positive thinkers who offer the promise of wealth, success, and health through their teachings. They believe that there is enough for everyone and if we just demonstrate our faith a little bit more, everything will be ours for the taking. These preachers repeat the same message in a variety of ways, but one thing is clear: the devil is negative thinking. Robert Schuller, a televangelist until he died in 2015, advised, "Never verbalize a negative emotion." Televangelist Joyce Meyer states that our attitude determines the kind of life we will have and that "It's especially important to maintain a positive attitude because God is positive." Within these positive religious communities, there is a strong belief that everything happens for a reason, it's all part of God's plan, if you had faith you wouldn't worry, and God wants you to be healthy, happy, and rich. If you are falling short in any of these areas, you simply need to change your thoughts.

As the rate of traditional religious affiliation declines, modern spirituality has become even more enticing. The Pew Research Center reported in 2019 that the number of American adults who describe themselves as Christian is down 12 percent over the past decade. Meanwhile, the percentage of people who describe themselves as atheist, agnostic, or "nothing" is up 9 percent in the same time period. Rates of religious attendance are also declining. Fifty-four percent of Americans say they attend religious services only a few times or less a year. Many of these people are leaving organized religion and turning to spirituality. Unfortunately, modern spirituality has also been taken over by consumer capitalism and positive thinking.

Toxic positivity in spirituality is often called "spiritual bypassing."

John Welwood coined the term and defined it as "using spiritual ideas and practices to sidestep personal, emotional 'unfinished business,' to shore up a shaky sense of self, or to belittle basic needs, feelings, and developmental tasks." Welwood noticed that many people were using spirituality as a way to avoid painful emotions and experiences. This continues today in many spiritual practices or communities worldwide that offer countless ways to create "unlimited" happiness and manifest everything you've ever wanted without ever acknowledging the internal and systemic barriers that may get in the way.

Mental Health and Religion Are Friends

Liz was really struggling with her mental health and her identity. Her religion was both a comfort and a burden for her. She felt shame and salvation simultaneously. For Liz, it felt like therapy and religion couldn't go together. She had trouble visualizing a life where she could hold on to her religion, maintain her true identity, and access the science-backed help she needed.

Research demonstrates that religious involvement has a preventative relationship in relation to psychological distress. This does not mean that religious people do not become ill and are always happy. It simply means that religion may be a productive and important coping skill for some people who are struggling. This is likely because of the inherent benefits that are found within a community. People who belong to a religious group will benefit from the promotion of health behaviors and opportunities for socialization with like-minded individuals. Faith and religious beliefs may also instill hope or optimism that is helpful in moments of distress.

When religious communities cultivate a community of acceptance, faith, and understanding, membership can be extremely beneficial. If we want to eliminate toxic positivity from religion, we have to focus on what we actually need and want from religion—a framework of hope, community, and a set of standards for living. Not another place that makes us feel less than or like we have to constantly pursue a better, improved version of ourselves to reach happiness.

Science and Positive Thinking

Scientific and psychological research have also been major contributors to the rise of toxic positivity. When Darwin's theory of evolution was popularized, there was a huge push to replace religion with science as the voice of authority. Researchers produced many "scientific studies" to prove that certain species do better because of biological differences—like a cheerful disposition and emotional self-control. Scientific experiments where treatment was withheld from people who had illnesses like alcoholism and tuberculosis were even used to test resilience and provide evidence for natural selection and survival of the fittest.

Looking back on this "science" may produce a sense of shock and horror today, but it's important to remember that these were the experts of the time. Their opinions, scientific inquiry, and assessments were believed and highly regarded within the scientific community. These beliefs were made even more popular due to the promise of happiness. Researchers and proponents of eugenics promised people that if we simply eliminated the weak and negative, those left behind would be free to pursue their best and happiest life. It was a promise that many could not ignore.

Today, science and research are still considered one of the most reliable and trustworthy sources of information, and often they are. Things have certainly changed and improved since the era of eugenics. However, when looking at how toxic positivity has endured over the past centuries, we have to look at the role of the scientific community and how positivity continues to be sold as the proven and well-researched key to happiness.

I saw the impact of this firsthand with Tory, whom you met in chapter one. She's one of those people who has truly tried it all and has been unable to achieve that elusive goal of happiness. The most interesting thing about Tory's wellness quest is that the majority of it claimed to be backed by scientific evidence and research. This led her to feel even more shame when things didn't work out the way she wanted them to. In our sessions, we talk about research and its limitations and how not everything that's reported will be true for all people because it has not been tried on all people in all situations (this includes everything I back up with research in this book). We discuss how science can be wrong and how we still need to use discretion and caution when applying it to our own lives. This is something that I hope you'll keep in mind when reading this book or other science-backed wellness strategies. Research is necessary, and it's usually quite helpful. But history also shows us how science has been used to maintain certain problematic aspects of the social order and framed them as part of the pursuit of "happiness."

Reflection

Take a moment to think about the messages you've heard about positivity in these areas and how they have impacted you.

- How has positive thinking been pushed in your workplace? Has it ever been used to cover up larger issues? What would make your workplace a more positive place to be?

- Has positivity ever been encouraged by healthcare professionals in your life? How did this impact your healing or the healing of a loved one?

- What is your relationship with religion or spirituality? Is positive thinking an integral part of your beliefs? How have those beliefs been formed by spiritual or religious leaders in your community?

Be happy
for all it
taught you.

You can be grateful for the lesson and still wish the event didn't happen.

....

Chapter Three

When Positivity Doesn't Help

Positivity can become toxic in several key situations. I have identified eleven different situations where positivity is likely to become toxic if used improperly. They are topics that I think we should all handle carefully and thoughtfully.

1. Infertility and Pregnancy Loss

Annie has had several pregnancy losses and is now struggling with infertility. She started seeing me after college and returned to therapy after her first miscarriage at seven weeks. Annie has her life together by most standards. She complains that she did "everything right" yet is still being punished. "I went to college and got the degree. I've never been arrested. I don't do drugs and I stopped drinking after my first loss. I have a job and a caring husband. What did I do to deserve this?" Annie is playing into a common theme that I see in therapy—the "just-world bias." It's a cognitive bias and fallacy that implies a person's actions will lead to morally fair and fitting consequences. It is the assumption that good things happen to good people and bad things happen to bad people. Believing in this gives us an illusion of control over life and often lets us justify inexplicable events. Annie is trying to understand why something so bad could happen to someone so good.

Her struggle has been met with well-intentioned but unhelpful support from the people around her. These are some of the most common words of encouragement she's received:

- "The baby you're meant to have will come."

- "God only gives you what you can handle."

- "At least there are so many other ways to make a family."

- "Think positive and the baby will come. If you're stressed, it won't work."

She knows they're just trying to help, but the positive sayings and words of encouragement leave her feeling alone, misunderstood, and afraid to share what she's feeling. Annie wants people to know that she felt each of these babies was meant for her and taken without her consent. She doesn't understand why any God would ever want to test her this way or make her feel how she's felt. Annie knows there are so many ways to make a family, and she's happy for the people that have chosen those ways. She never expresses judgment toward people who have adopted or used a surrogate, but Annie wants to be pregnant. She wants to experience what other women she knows have. She wants that experience and it's her right to grieve that loss if and when she needs to. I know that Annie tried thinking positively because she did it in my office. She attempted to put a positive spin on those initial losses, every doctor appointment, and every new attempt to conceive. She tried when every doctor told her that stress and negativity would stop her from getting pregnant. She blamed herself for not being positive after each loss and swore she would manage her stress better next time. Annie tried so hard to see the bright side until she just couldn't anymore.

Annie and I talked about what she wished people had done or told her during the countless doctor appointments, new treatments, and after each loss. This is what she told me:

- "That is so painful/hard."

- "Do you want to talk about it? I'm here to listen."

- "I'm dropping off dinner for you tonight."

- Sent a text before or after an important appointment to check in.

- Not taken it personally if she didn't respond for a while. It wasn't them.

- "This loss matters and it makes sense that you're grieving."

- "I know how much you want this. I'm here to support you through every step."

2. Grief and Loss

The Fernandez family enters my office on Tuesday morning for an emergency session after their twenty-three-year-old son was tragically killed in a boating accident over the weekend. Each member is showing their grief in a unique and personal way. The teenage sister is fidgeting in her chair, completely silent, as her eyes dart around the room. The mother is quiet and keeps her gaze pointed at the floor while the father sobs uncontrollably into his hands, his whole body quaking with each sob. The younger brother tries to comfort his father by scooting closer and patting his back. They're all hurting and I sit there staring back at them; no amount of training or experience makes these moments less challenging.

The father's sobs start to slow down after a few minutes and I take this as a sign that I can begin the session. I begin by asking them all how they're doing and giving each member of the family time to share and be heard. They're each questioning the meaning of life, desperate for answers, and in indescribable pain. We talk about how they're managing their pain and what support they can access within their community. The teenage sister shares that they haven't been very religious and attended their local temple occasionally on high holidays. They're wondering if they should start going to temple. "Will that help?" she pleads. I know they want me to give them a manual on how to grieve, and I also know I won't be able to do that. This is my biggest weakness as a therapist. I know I have to keep checking in and reminding myself that this is the work, being here, holding this space for them, and letting them feel. There is no manual.

The father mentions that several members of their congregation at temple tried to offer words of encouragement. They were saying things like:

- "It was all part of God's plan."

- "They're in a better place."

- "They wouldn't want to see you sad."

- "You need to be strong for your kids."

- "This teaches you to always be grateful for what you have."

- "Everything happens for a reason."

Like Annie, he knows they're just trying to help, but he doesn't understand how taking his child could be part of God's plan. The mother can't understand how anywhere could be better than their son being with their family here in Miami. They share how whatever lesson this is supposed to teach them will never be worth the loss of their child and will never make sense. We talk about how it's good for the other children to see their parents express difficult emotions and handle them. I help them navigate the definition of "strong" and how to be strong when dealing with such immense and tragic loss. Ultimately, the family agrees that these words, while well-intentioned, left them feeling like they were doing this grief thing wrong. They simply couldn't find a single way to put a positive spin on the unexpected loss of their son on a sunny Saturday afternoon.

The Fernandez family's complaints about these statements aren't unique. It's something I've heard from countless families dealing with grief and loss. Here are some suggestions that might be more helpful for someone grieving a loss:

- "I'm sorry you are going through this loss. I'm here and I will listen if you want to talk about it."

- Check in on them with a text or call.

- Respect their boundaries if they aren't ready to talk about it, don't want certain help, etc.

- Listen and affirm how much the grief hurts.

- Ask them about the deceased or the person they no longer have in their life. Give them space to talk about them and share memories or stories.

- "I don't know what to say, but I'm here for you."

3. Illness and Disability

I believe that no one is encouraged to just "be positive" more than those with chronic illness, disabilities, and health issues. I've worked with this population for my entire career, but Michael's story has always stayed with me. Michael is a transgender male who lives with several mental and physical health diagnoses. He has been dealing with an onslaught of mysterious symptoms since age twelve. This means he has had countless opportunities for gaslighting and dismissal within the medical system and among his family, friends, and peers.

Michael and I meet online using video because it's much more manageable when he has a symptom flare. For this session, Michael is in his bed and I can tell this is probably the only interaction he's going to be able to manage today. We spend many of our sessions processing his recent appointments, managing the isolation of living with chronic illness, and adapting to life in a slowly declining body. Michael has recently been on the receiving end of some egregious toxic positivity in an online community for alternative healing methods, and he's fired up. He knows how much I hate this stuff, so we're having a good time discussing what's been said and how it's dismissive or unhelpful. Michael has worked extensively on his identity as a trans male with chronic illness and is typically not offended or reactive when he reads these statements, but he knows how damaging they were early on in his journey. He shared some of the worst statements he's seen:

- "But look at all you can do!"

- "You need to have a good attitude if you want to beat this!"

- "My friend had this and they got better, so I know you will, too!"

- "Gosh, this really reminds you how precious life is and how we should be grateful for what we have."

- "You're so brave."

- "Maybe you need to try yoga or juicing? It's helped me so much!"

- "You don't even look sick. You look great!"

Michael and I discussed the value of looking at the things you can do and being grateful for that, but how this statement is also dismissive because it doesn't attend to or affirm the pain and loss of living with illness. He shared the dangers of telling someone they'll get better or pressuring them to try a treatment just because a friend did, and I agree with him. It's something I've seen among many of my clients with chronic illnesses. Giving out medical advice or suggestions is pretty much always well-intentioned, but it can be dangerous or provide false hope. That second one, "You need to have a good attitude if you want to beat this!" is the most common one, and Michael and I laugh as a way to cope with the irony of this statement. Just like Annie, this person believes in the just-world bias. They think that people who think positive thoughts get positive outcomes, like guaranteed health. If anyone knows this isn't true for everyone, it's smiley, happy, upbeat Michael, who has slowly lost his zest for life as his health declines and the world moves on without him.

What Michael has experienced and witnessed in this online community is the reality for so many chronically ill and disabled people. Unfortunately, the excessive emphasis on positive thinking can lead to victim blaming and shaming in healthcare. It implies that those who work hard enough and have the right attitude always win in the fight for health. The people who are negative always lose. We all know this just isn't the reality. Here are some things Michael wishes people said or did instead:

- "I'm here for you."

- "I believe you."

- "I'll go with you to your next appointment if that would be helpful."

- "I read about your diagnosis and I'm learning about _____."

- "Have any of your symptoms changed today?"

- "I'll always be here no matter what happens."

- "You know your body best."

4. Romantic Relationship Struggles

Pedro is a fifty-four-year-old male who recently finalized his divorce from his partner of twenty years. On a good day, his relationship was exciting and passionate. But I would classify it as toxic, verbally abusive, and hostile on its worst days. Pedro struggled immensely with leaving his partner and was met with a lot of resistance from his Cuban Catholic family. We briefly tried couples therapy, but there was no remorse or recognition of the abuse from his partner. I told Pedro that couples therapy would be futile and possibly even dangerous while his relationship was in this state. He decided to move forward with individual therapy and his partner was happy to opt out.

Pedro had a lot of deeply ingrained beliefs about commitment, marriage, and love. Every time he tried to share his feelings about his divorce with his family or friends, they further solidified these beliefs. Before he decided to pursue a divorce, people would say things to him like:

- "The right one will never leave you or hurt you."

- "At least you have someone."

- "Love means sacrifice."

- "Other relationships are worse. Be grateful for what he does for you!"

- "All you need is love. Love will get you through this."

We talked about how these statements made Pedro doubt and dismiss the verbal abuse he had experienced throughout his relationship. It made it so difficult for him to trust himself and his experience. It also kept him trapped in a relationship where he was deeply unhappy and constantly belittled.

After the divorce was finalized and Pedro was newly single, he continued therapy to process the end of his relationship and the grief that followed. He noticed that post-divorce, he was on the receiving end of an entirely different type of pressure. Now people wanted him to look on the bright side and make the best out of his new situation. Everyone was saying things like:

- "No one will love you until you love yourself."

- "Enjoy being single. I would kill to have that freedom again."

- "This is what you wanted."

- "People love positive and happy people. The right attitude will help you find the right person."

It was like he had just crossed the finish line for one race and now people were demanding he run another with a smile. Pedro couldn't keep up with the requests to make the best of his abusive relationship and now to make the best of his new single life. He was grieving, lonely, and unsure of what his future held.

This is how toxic positivity shows up for those struggling with romantic relationships. We want people to be happy alone and happy together—no matter what that looks like or forces them to endure. The fairy-tale love myth continues to persist. We propose that people who are single are surely only that way because they're miserable or not trying hard enough. Relationships that end just ran out of love, weren't meant to be, or someone simply wasn't trying hard enough. These perspectives silence victims who are enduring real abuse in their relationships and make being single something to be avoided like the plague. Here's what Pedro wishes people said or did instead:

- "I believe you."

- "It must be so hard to be alone after all these years."

- Invite him to do something or check in.

- "Relationships are complicated. I trust that you're doing what is right for you."

- "I love you."

- "Your worth isn't determined by your relationship status."

5. Family and Family Estrangement

Maggie is one of those clients who comes to therapy only when there's a crisis. I've been seeing her for years and we meet for a few weeks every time something happens in her family. After a few sessions, she usually reports feeling grounded and in touch with her values again. She puts a pause on therapy, and I subtly encourage her to continue attending so we can get deeper into the issue and then wait for her to reach out again in a few months.

Maggie sends me a panicked email one afternoon after her mother sent her a "disturbing" email. She's not sure how to respond and needs a session, so I fit her in the next week. Maggie's mother has been a constant issue throughout her life. The drinking, yelling, nonstop criticism, and complete lack of accountability are just things that Maggie eventually learned to deal with. She thought all moms were like this until she started spending time around her husband's family. Maggie and I have been working on boundaries, not normalizing problematic behavior, and communicating her needs. She's made major improvements. But every once in a while, her mom reappears and violates a boundary or accuses Maggie of something she had no part in. This week it's an email accusing her of being selfish and stealing money from her mom's bank account. Despite her extensive boundary work, it hurts whenever Maggie receives messages like this from her mom. It takes her right back to her childhood and she has to pause before reacting.

Over the years, Maggie has contemplated completely cutting her mother out of her life. A few years ago, an incident left her feeling like she couldn't do this anymore. The problem is, every time she considers doing this or takes a step in that direction, she gets so much pushback from other members of her family. They flood her with toxic positivity like:

- "Family is everything."

- "She can't be that bad."

- "I could never cut my mom out of my life! I love her."

- "Blood is thicker than water."

- "You should be grateful for everything your mother has done for you. She did her best."

They're always urging her to see the good in her mom and to be just a little bit more forgiving. Some of them deny that the relationship is even toxic. It has left her feeling totally isolated, misunderstood, and like she's a drama queen.

What Maggie is experiencing is common for so many families. We want to believe that family members will always treat us well and that they love us, but this just isn't the case. When estranged family members or victims of abuse are forced to look on the bright side or accept toxic behavior "because it's family," we further victimize and isolate them. I think Maggie would've been able to recognize the abuse she endured and set boundaries much more quickly if she'd had more external support. This is what she would've liked to hear instead:

- "That must have been a tough decision to make."

- "I know that you are doing what is best for you."

- "I support your decision."

- "I won't ever judge you for making that choice."

- "I'm here if you ever want to talk about it."

6. Career Trouble or Job Loss

Alissa and I are meeting for another session today. It's the middle of summer and the sun is beating in through the windows at eight thirty in the morning. Alissa schedules her sessions before work; otherwise, she'll end up canceling them when the day gets away from her. Today, Alissa's tone is slightly different. She shares that she wants to quit her job. I pause for a minute and allow the silence to fill the room around us. Alissa begins to speak again: "I just can't do this anymore."

You may remember when Alissa shared with her boss that she wasn't sleeping and was very overwhelmed. Her boss responded with, "Be grateful you have the work. People would kill to have this job." This is the standard toxic positivity that Alissa gets in the workplace from her coworkers and superiors whenever she wants to bring up real issues in the office or just vent. She also hears a lot of:

- "Positive people always succeed."

- "You just need to try harder!"

- "Your attitude determines how successful you will be."

- "If you want to make it to the top, you need to be willing to sacrifice."

- "That's just the job. You knew what you were getting yourself into."

These statements go great with the required burnout training and no actual support to fix the burnout, the doughnuts at the late-night meetings, and the chocolate candies at Christmas when she's working fourteen-hour days. They want her to be happy, positive, and successful but won't give her the support she needs to get there—or the necessary hours of sleep. Here's what Alissa and her coworkers wish was actually said and done:

- "I hear your complaints and am going to meet with management to find a way to make this work for everyone."

- Adequate pay and reasonable work hours that allow for balance outside of work.

- "Work has been really difficult lately. Thank you for all your support. I'll make sure you get a break when this project is done."

- "Thank you for bringing up that important issue. We value our employees' opinions and feelings. Let's find a way to work on this."

- Fewer parties and trainings, more actual support with work, paid time off, and fair deadlines.

7. Physical Appearance

Almost all of my female clients have discussed issues with their appearance or body in therapy. Leah is one of them. Leah has struggled with her body image for as long as she can remember. She's a yo-yo dieter who often gets sucked into the latest diet craze or beauty treatment. Leah is desperate for improvement and pursues beauty at all costs. Her diet behaviors completely control her psychologically and prevent her from living a full and meaningful life. Each month there are new restrictions on where and what she can eat.

Leah has a habit of bringing up her body concerns with the people around her in an attempt to reassure herself. I hear women do this all the time—myself included. "God, my butt has gotten so big!" or "I seriously look so bad today. I need to work out." We tear ourselves down publicly so that others will reassure us. It's a vicious cycle and it rarely works. Whenever Leah complains about her weight or size to friends or family, they usually respond with comments like:

- "No, you haven't gained weight at all! You look amazing!"

- "If you gained weight, you seriously can't tell at all!"

- "You look so skinny!"

- "I would kill to have a body like yours! Look at my (insert body part you don't like)."

These exchanges and "compliments" always reaffirm for Leah that being thin is ideal. Her friends are seemingly trying to reassure her that she is still living in the "best" type of body and she shouldn't be worried. Their comments are well-intentioned and kind, but Leah and I discuss how all they seem to do is reinforce the idea that being thin is the goal and avoiding weight gain is mandatory.

In our sessions, we talk a lot about "body neutrality." You've probably heard of body positivity, which can quickly become another form of toxic positivity; this is different. While body positivity pushes us to love our bodies and find joy in every bump, dimple, or curve, body neutrality allows you to make peace with the body you have. It is the idea that you can exist without having to think too much about your body or view it as positive or negative. Your body is just your body; some days you're going to like parts or all of it, and other days you may struggle, but it's still just your body. Despite the overwhelming presence of the body positivity movement online and the introduction of body neutrality, the quest to stay thin continues to be a pressing issue for so many people. We are bombarded with diet culture at every turn and this billion-dollar industry tries its absolute best to keep us enthralled with the idea of being "healthy" or thin. Leah struggles with this, I have certainly struggled with it, and maybe you have, too.

Instead of celebrating only certain bodies, we can all learn to be a little more neutral and compassionate to our own bodies and others. Leah and I discussed compliments that have nothing to do with weight or physical appearance and how she can redirect the conversation whenever someone is engaging in toxic positivity or just bashing themselves. Here are some different statements we came up with in session:

- Compliment something that isn't body- or physical appearance–related, like a facet of their personality or something they accomplished.

- If someone is speaking negatively about their own body, it's OK to shut down the conversation or change the subject.

- Try to speak about what your body does for you (i.e., "I was able to hike the entire trail today.") instead of focusing on how many calories you burned or how an activity is going to improve your body (i.e., "That hike was so hard. I bet I earned a cheeseburger tonight. Maybe I'll be bad and get one.").

- When someone complains about their body, instead of complimenting them, try to change the subject or ask why they might be feeling that way. It may also be helpful to say, "I also feel bad about my body sometimes and I'm trying to work on that." This helps normalize how they're feeling without minimizing it or covering it up with a compliment.

- Try to spend time talking about topics other than food, calories, diets, and your body. Notice when your friends and family do this and how it sounds or makes you feel.

8. After a Traumatic Event

James sent me a cryptic email on a Sunday evening asking for more information about therapy. The email made it obvious that James didn't want me to think he was "sick" or really "needed" services. I called him for a phone consultation and discovered just how much he had been suffering for the last several years. When James was a teenager, an intruder broke into his home, robbed his family, and harmed his younger brother sleeping in the bed next to him. He had been experiencing vivid flashbacks, insomnia, and intrusive thoughts since the incident five years ago. He described the event as being "not that big of a deal" and something he "should be over by now," but it was clear the event had a large impact on his overall functioning and sense of safety.

After the break-in, James tried talking about it with friends and his parents. They all told him he'd get over it or some version of that:

- "Wow, you're so brave!"

- "Think about all you learned."

- "At least you're all alive. You can replace things."

- "Everything happens for a reason. You'll get through this."

Just like the Fernandez family, who lost their son in a boating accident, James is having a lot of trouble understanding why this happened and what he learned other than a constant feeling of being unsafe. Yes, he's grateful he and his family are alive, but he also wishes his brother hadn't been impacted and that their home still felt safe. James was a teenager; he didn't want to be brave, he wanted to be a kid.

I use a therapy modality called Eye Movement Desensitization and Reprocessing (EMDR) with James to help him eliminate the flashbacks and feel safe in his body again. We spend every other session using a light bar that he follows with his eyes and audio and tactile stimulation. James focuses on the distressing mental image of an intruder in his home and the details that follow. We are working on integrating the traumatic memory and making it less distressing for James. After each EMDR session, we spend time processing how his symptoms are impacting him. James talks a lot about how he wishes his family and friends could have supported him more in the aftermath of this traumatic experience. Here is what he wishes they would have done instead:

- Validate how he was feeling without minimizing it. "I get why you would feel scared. That is scary."

- Sit with him and listen to how he was feeling.

- Respect his boundaries—especially if he wasn't ready to talk or didn't want to share a certain detail.

- Focus less on why it happened and what he might have learned. Instead, focus on how he was feeling and how it impacted him.

- Remember that even though the event was over, he was still being impacted by it.

9. Pregnancy and Parenting

Pregnancy and parenting are hard. I've found that no one really speaks openly about how absolutely challenging it is to grow and raise a human. I am five months pregnant while writing this chapter and have experienced a lot of the toxic positivity that gets thrown at pregnant people and parents. As soon as you share that you're pregnant, the opinions, warnings, and demands for gratitude start following from every source—family, friends, social media, advertisements, and more. Like many people growing a human, I have engaged in my fair share of complaining about nausea, aches, and ever-stretching skin. Here are some classic toxic positivity statements I've received:

- "Enjoy every minute."

- "Just wait. You'll want this time back."

- "Be grateful you are able to have children."

- "Every child is a gift."

- "There are so many people out there who would want to be in your shoes."

- "Pregnancy is always such a magical time."

It hurts whenever I'm looking for support or affirmation and someone responds with a comment like this. I know they're trying to help, but guilt just floods my body. I start beating myself up and shut down—not wanting to ask anyone for support for fear of appearing ungrateful or rejected. This sentiment has been echoed by so many of my pregnant and parent clients. There's an immense pressure to be grateful for every facet of parenthood, and not doing so makes you a bad or ungrateful parent. We've got to change the narrative here.

I can honestly say I have been grateful for every day of my pregnancy but, gosh, on those days where I was slumped over a toilet for hours and holding back vomit while sitting across from a vulnerable client who had no idea, it was so hard. On the days when my skin is stretching and my husband wants to touch me, I think I'll scream if he does. In these moments, it is so hard for me to be grateful. It's hard for me to see this child as a gift when I wake up every thirty minutes to pee even though I haven't had any water. Despite all this, I am immensely grateful for this baby and this pregnancy. So here's what I wish people did for me instead and some suggestions I've heard from my clients:

- Let me vent without forcing gratitude. I promise I am grateful.

- Don't use the fact that other people can't get pregnant as a way to bring me down to earth. I know I am lucky. It doesn't make this hurt any less.

- Validate how I'm feeling and know that I'm just going through a moment. "Wow, that does sound painful" works really well.

- Just show up and be supportive. Drop off a meal, send a text, or offer to do the laundry.

- Remember that every single pregnancy is different. What may have been magical for you is utterly excruciating for someone else.

10. Racism, Homophobia, Sexism, Ableism, Sizeism, Classism, and Other Types of Prejudice

The internet and social media have become an increasingly tense space over the last four years. But after George Floyd's death in May 2020, the Web exploded. Voices shouted over one another as people angrily (and justifiably) pounded their keyboards demanding answers and justice. The noise was dizzying and I watched as something really interesting unfolded. Toxic positivity was literally everywhere, and it was mainly white people or people who had never been impacted by this type of injustice shouting it through their tiny phone screens into the black hole of the internet. The comments rolled in:

- "Can't we all just love each other?!"

- "Let's just all get along!"

- "We need peace."

- "We're all just one human race."

- "I don't see color. I love everyone the same!"

Yes, it would be wonderful if we all loved each other. It's a goal I'd like to achieve, too. It would also be great if we could all just get along and have more peace. And technically, yes, we are all one human race. But is this the most helpful and productive way to respond right now?

I will never pretend to be an expert on antiracism, racism, or any other aspect of prejudice. I've learned a lot from some amazing teachers and leaders in that arena and I suspect I'll be learning and messing up for a long time. I do feel very confident about how we should be responding to people when they are experiencing real, measurable, and obvious forms of prejudice and discrimination. I know that responding in this way when someone is upset is dismissive and ultimately does nothing. If you've said some of the statements listed above, it's OK. Take a pause and a deep breath. It doesn't mean you're a bad person. As with any type of toxic positivity, the intention is often good, but the impact really stings and, in some cases, can cause real harm. This is about recognizing it and thinking about why it might not be helpful.

The core of toxic positivity is that it's dismissive and it shuts down the conversation. It effectively says, "Nope, that feeling you're experiencing, it's wrong—and here's why you should be happy instead." It's the exact opposite of what we want to do when people are in pain. When talking about racism or any other type of prejudice with people who are struggling or who have experience living with that identity, we want to make space, validate them, and then take action on our own to fight against the systems that have led us here. We need to be especially willing to do this when we have zero personal experience or insight into what it's like to live life in that body. This is one of those moments where it's good to defer to the experts. Not every group of people who are marginalized or struggling feels the same. Every person who is disabled or living in a larger body or is a person of color will have a slightly different experience; they are not a monolithic group. This is when it's so important that we put the platitudes away and listen.

I have learned some things that we can do and say in lieu of those statements from wonderful antiracist educators in the community. Erin Matthews, LCSW, Rachel Cargle, and Tarana J. Burke are a few of the many educators who have provided me with endless amounts of education. I have also learned from so many other individuals who are fighting against sexism, homophobia, ableism, sizeism, and other types of prejudice within our communities. My biggest takeaway from this education is that talk is cheap and platitudes are even cheaper. We have to learn how to act.

The next time you feel compelled to use toxic positivity in response to someone's struggle in one or more of these areas, you can use one of these suggestions I have gathered instead:

- Listen to people with lived experience and say, "I believe you."

- Do your own research. Find books, websites, podcasts, etc. to educate yourself on what it's like to embody one of these many marginalized groups.

- Have conversations with friends, family, and coworkers about these topics.

- Follow influencers online who are a part of these groups.

- Support businesses owned by marginalized individuals.

- Pay employees fairly and have adequate representation in the workplace.

- Hold businesses accountable for their prejudice.

- Vote for legislation and leaders that support these individuals.

- Admit when you're wrong and create a plan to do better.

- Remind yourself that this is a never-ending process.

This is, of course, not an exhaustive list and there is so much more to be done here, but it's a great place to start. We'll get into how toxic positivity continues to prop up these systems in chapter eight.

11. Mental Health Issues

Liz struggled with anxiety and tried to reconcile her faith in God with her need for mental health treatment. She finally worked up the courage to tell her parents about therapy, but it took us many sessions to get to that point. Liz and I discussed her parents and how their beliefs impact her anxiety in one of those sessions. For them, getting mental health treatment was a sign of a lack of faith and strongly discouraged.

Liz's parents were constantly saying things like:

- "You're not sick!"

- "You have everything you need. What could you possibly be anxious about?"

- "You have so much to be grateful for and happy about. Focus on that."

- "Think happier thoughts and this will all get better."

- "You just need to be more positive."

These types of statements are common among people who don't fully understand the nature or complexity of mental health issues. To them, your mind is just something you get control of and fix with faith and a better attitude. It doesn't make sense to them that someone could be really trying to be happy or less anxious and still be unable to snap out of it.

Mental health issues are really complicated and there's rarely one cause. As a therapist, I've noticed that no one wants to get better more than the patient who is struggling with these issues. I have never met a therapy client who truly enjoys struggling with their mental health and doesn't want it to get better. I know from the outside it might not look that way, but it's true. They are usually terrified, don't know where to start, or don't understand how anything could ever be different.

Watching someone struggle with their mental health is challenging. It can make you feel like you're drowning and unable to save someone you care about. This forces us to try all sorts of things, like toxic positivity, in an attempt to help. Liz understood that her parents had good intentions and she knew they wanted to help. Here's what she wishes they would have done or said instead:

- "I believe you and I know you don't want to feel this way."

- "I can see how hard you're trying."

- "I support you and am here to help."

- Sit with her in moments when she was really struggling.

- Learn more about what she was dealing with through research and asking questions.

- Acknowledge that even people who have it all can still struggle with their mental health.

Reflection

- Have there been situations in your life where positivity was unhelpful?

- Have there been situations in your life where positivity was helpful?

- If you've dealt with any of these eleven situations, how did you want to be supported or helped?

- How has this chapter helped you understand the different ways people like to be supported?

So many people have it worse. Be grateful for what you have.

··

There will always be someone who has it worse and someone who has it better. Recognizing that something is worse may help give you perspective, but it doesn't diminish what you're feeling. It's OK to complain about something you're grateful for.

. . . .

Chapter Four

Stop Shaming Yourself

I mastered the art of pretending at a young age. Not the kind of pretending where you put on a dress and make-believe you're a princess; this was different. This pretending involved walking on eggshells and hiding anything that wasn't perfect or beautiful. It was buying a new wardrobe when you're sad and denying the sadness even existed. There was always a new purchase, event, or trip to cover up and make up for the existence of every single negative emotion. I learned that if you were going to be sad, you better have a good enough reason. I also became acutely aware that you weren't allowed to be sad if you had things and resources. Someone always had it worse and that was reason enough to deny, deny, deny.

It became apparent that there were "good" and "bad" feelings. It didn't matter what was going on in life; you got dressed, put on a smile, and got the job done. If someone hurt you and you tried to bring that up, you were being "negative." As long as everyone believed you were happy, you were happy. I realized the goal wasn't to actually be happy, but to appear happy.

So many of us get stuck in this trap. We're trying to look happy on social media before we actually address how we feel inside. When people ask us how we're feeling we lie and say "Great!" with a forced smile. We pretend because we think it's what we have to do. We're terrified of what will happen if we stop pretending. Will I scare them away? Will they be able to handle how I really feel? Best not to risk it, right?

Looking back, I spent so much of my life pretending. Pretending I was happy, pretending I felt confident, pretending I liked my body. It became second nature, like flipping a switch. Honestly, I think that's why I am so disillusioned with the litany of perfect photos on Instagram and I struggle being around people who act happy all the time. It's like I know their secret. For a while, I really believed pretending was the only way to live. I told myself I had financial security so I couldn't be sad. I was in a "normal" body so I couldn't hate it. I went to a good school so I couldn't complain. "I have so much to be thankful for, other people have it worse, and I should be happy." These became the messages echoing endlessly in my head. A mountain of forced gratitude was poured on top of every single distressing

Feeling depressed or anxious is hard. Pretending that you're not is much harder.

emotion I felt until I literally couldn't breathe. Feeling depressed or anxious is hard. Pretending that you're not is much harder.

In my midtwenties I realized I was completely and utterly exhausted from pretending. I found myself struggling to keep up the facade. I became blatantly honest about my feelings; some would say too honest. I couldn't be around anyone who was faking their joy. I started noticing how I was showing up on social media and how it totally contradicted what I was feeling inside. I saw this in others, too. The friend that was crying over a breakup and posting ten smiling selfies with the caption "Life is awesome!" The mom who hadn't spoken to her kids in a month and put up a picture saying "I just love my kids!" And the many, many smiling faces that stared back at me as I scrolled through image after image on Instagram. It wasn't the fact that people were happy on social media or that they weren't being vulnerable with all their followers. Public vulnerability and sharing all your feelings with the world isn't required. It was the complete incongruence between the state of their real life and what they were showing to the world. There was pressure to show up one way publicly and hide everything else. This realization meant ending relationships and a lot of growing pains. Toxic positivity was slowly losing its grip on me.

I naively thought I was the only one who felt this way, but we're rarely alone in how we feel. Client after client sat on my couch and told me about the toxic positivity in their lives. The well-intentioned messages from friends and family, the work happy hours at their soul-sucking jobs, and the pressure to look like they had it all together. I often wonder what my clients' social media pages look like (I've never looked because, well, ethics). But I found myself asking: Did it completely contradict what they shared in therapy? How much of what they put out there did they actually believe? Did they just want others to believe it?

When I first started my training to become a therapist, I noticed there was such a big focus on positive thinking and positive emotions. We learned about difficult emotions from a mental illness perspective and the goal was to shift the negative emotions into positive ones. I wanted to eradicate suffering completely, not learn how to live with it and deal with it. I know I was handing out toxic positivity like candy with my first clients. If you're reading this, I'm sorry. I thought it was what you needed. My clients were tired of hiding their feelings from friends, tired of putting on a smile at work, and tired of posting photos on Instagram after crying alone in the bathroom. Over time, it became glaringly evident that we were all sick and tired of toxic positivity and everyone was too afraid to say anything. Honestly, I was just happy not to be alone.

How We Use Toxic Positivity Against Ourselves

This is what toxic positivity does to us. It traps us in a life of pretending until we can't do it anymore. It tells us that if someone has it worse, we can't be sad. If there's something to be grateful for, gratitude must be the only emotion. It tells you that you should be happy and that you should be over this by now. It leaves you hiding behind a mass of fake joy, isolated and alone. Toxic positivity increases feelings of shame, inadequacy, and isolation. It might originate from good intentions, but it doesn't do us any favors.

We use toxic positivity against ourselves when we say things like:

- "I should be over this by now."

- "I should be happy."

- "I have so much to be grateful for."

- "Other people have it worse."

- "I shouldn't be feeling like this. My life is so full."

- "Other people would love to have my problems. It's not that bad."

Toxic positivity harms us in so many ways, including:

- Ending the curiosity and exploration of the emotion

- Shaming you for being "negative"

- Making you not want to reach out to others

- Suppressing emotion and making it more intense and harder to manage

Toxic positivity tells us that what we're feeling is wrong and that we shouldn't be feeling it. It demands that we have a "good enough" reason for any type of distress. When we believe that there are certain emotions that we should feel and others that we shouldn't, we're doomed to experience shame when we experience more of the latter and less of the former. This is why we end up trying to suppress and cover up all of our difficult emotions with shopping, food, alcohol, social media, and any other form of numbing we can get our hands on. We want to exit the distress as soon as possible so we can avoid the shame of feeling it in the first place. Shaming ourselves for experiencing a normal, biologically programmed response to a stimulus isn't going to lead us anywhere. It's just going to end in more shame, pretending, and hiding.

When we use toxic positivity against ourselves, it obstructs curiosity and exploration of the emotion. Think about it. When you're feeling sad and someone says "just be happy," are you going to keep talking about how sad you are? No. You're probably going to shut down and end the conversation. We're trying to deny the existence of an emotion because it doesn't line up with what we think should be there. But here's the thing: emotions aren't intellectual. You can't think them away or deny them out of existence. Emotions don't always tell the truth and sometimes we interpret them incorrectly, but they're there for a reason. Telling yourself that you shouldn't be feeling something won't change that reality.

Whenever I tried to cover up what I was feeling with positivity,

I was always left with guilt or shame or both. Guilt tells us that we did something bad; shame says we are bad. When we condemn ourselves for having a feeling or try to cover it up with positive thinking and gratitude, it leaves us feeling ashamed, isolated, and afraid to share our feelings with anyone else. If everyone else is happy, we should be, too. If we have negative feelings, well, then there must be something wrong with us.

Toxic positivity also completely inhibits connection. If I believe that everyone else is happy (because that's what they're telling me and showing me) and I'm struggling, you better believe I'm not telling anyone. Because if I tell them that I'm not OK, I assume that will lead to judgment or criticism. It's so hard to connect when we feel isolated and like we're the only one experiencing something. Toxic positivity tells us that we should be happy all the time and anything else is a failure. But what if we're all feeling so many things and we're doing it alone when we don't have to? What if we're all a lot more alike in our distress than we are different? If I know that you also feel pain, it would make it a lot easier for me to share my struggles and my successes. It would really take the pressure off and allow me to just be.

Why Those Positive Affirmations Aren't Working

I went to a therapist when I was seventeen. In the second session he made me stand in front of a mirror and say positive affirmations to myself like "I love myself" and "I am worthy." I never went back to see him.

Honestly, positive affirmations have always felt a little forced, inauthentic, and awkward for me. I've tried them over the years because people rave about them, and I just always felt worse. It was hard for me to encourage my clients to use them after my own personal experience.

If you're in a really dark place, positive affirmations can feel like bold-faced lies. I've found that no one wants to admit this. It's like we're told over and over that positive thinking should work and will work, so we just keep repeating "I'm the best! I love myself!" and looking around the room thinking: *Is this really working for you? Am I doing something wrong?*

I'm not denying the power of language. Language is extremely important and it's a huge part of the work I do with clients. Every time I write about this, someone inevitably tells me that I need to do my research on the power of positive thinking and language. Yes, the science is very clear that positive language has a positive impact on us in some situations, and negative language can have a negative impact on us psychologically and physically. But it's not so black-and-white.

Positive thinking and positive affirmations have been shown to be more effective in subjects with higher self-esteem. For people with lower self-esteem, positive thinking is actually counterproductive. These people eventually realize that the words don't feel true and this can lead to more depression. Hyper-optimism also has been found to carry an additional risk of depression because hyper-optimists have been shown to lack preparation when confronted with risk or a difficult situation.

It's not as simple as: positive affirmation on repeat = happiness.

There are a few key reasons why positive affirmations may not be working for you:

If you think your positive affirmation isn't true, it's not going to work.

Let's say your goal is to love yourself. That would be nice, but you're not going to feel that love every day. "Loving yourself" is also quite an ambiguous goal. You may not really know what it means. There are still probably going to be things that get to you, days where you don't feel great, and times where you look in the mirror and negative thoughts pour in. If you are in a place where you really don't like or respect yourself, loving yourself might seem impossible. If you think the goal is to always love yourself, you're going to feel like a failure on the days when that positive affirmation is harder to integrate.

If you hate yourself and start repeating "I love myself" over and over, it might feel good for a moment. But pretty soon it will just be noise. It will start to feel false and empty. If you're anything like the hundreds of people who have shared this exact scenario with me, you'll probably start to feel like a failure. It's not your fault. The affirmation was just too much of a stretch for this moment.

If there's no behavioral change with the affirmation, it's not going to work.
The affirmation has to be backed up by action that informs the belief. If you are continuing to engage in behaviors that deny this belief or are completely opposed to it, it will become even more difficult to integrate the positive affirmation.

We have to look at both our thoughts and our behaviors. It's a great practice to ask yourself: *How can I act out this affirmation? How can I show myself what I want to believe?*

If we continue with the affirmation "I love myself," I would want to know:

- What does loving yourself look like?

- How can I show that I love myself? What behaviors would demonstrate that belief?

- How will I show myself love even when it's hard?

If there's no effort to create internal acceptance, love, and self-respect, it's not going to work.
When we use affirmations, we're trying to reach a place of love, acceptance, and self-respect for ourselves. In order to believe an

affirmation, we have to believe we are worthy of kindness. If you still hold on to a core belief that you're not worthy of love or kindness, the affirmation will ring hollow. We have to really believe that there is a possibility for this affirmation and other positive things about us to be true.

I find that it's helpful to start with the possibility of something being true and to create flexibility with the affirmation. So, if you want to love yourself, this is how you would make the affirmation more flexible and believable when acceptance, love, and self-respect are hard to find.

Instead of saying "I love myself," you would say:

- "I can learn to love myself."

- "I accept that I won't love myself every day."

- "I will try to show myself love even when it is hard."

- "If I can't love myself today, I will try again tomorrow."

- "Sometimes loving myself is hard and I am still trying."

When we open up room for compassion and possibility, we're creating mental flexibility. This allows us to have compassion when the affirmation doesn't feel true and to make room for the possibility that one day it will be true.

How to Make Affirmations Work for You

Language is incredibly powerful and important. If you create the right affirmations, they will help you achieve your goals and boost your mental health. An affirmation is something that you're repeating to yourself often and using when you're feeling great and feeling low. What could be more important than the way you speak to yourself all day long? Affirmations can be about how we would like to feel about ourselves, a goal, or just an overall feeling. Some examples: "I am resilient," "I am learning to love myself," "I know my own reality."

Affirmations work best when they are:

- in line with your current values

- truthful

- achievable

- backed up with real action

- used to empower and not to cover up or eliminate a distressing feeling

First, let's talk about how to align your affirmations with your values. Your values are the things that are most important in your life. They determine your priorities and how you tell if your life is going how you want it to. When your behavior is in line with your values, life usually feels pretty satisfying. When your values and actions are out of alignment, it becomes harder to get through the day. Research shows us that affirmations work best when they support your already existing values. This means that identifying your values is an important step when deciding on an affirmation.

To align your affirmations with your values, ask yourself:

- What are my core values? (A quick Google search will give you some great values lists.)

- What is important to me?

- How do my values show up in my daily life? Where do I tend to spend the most time and energy?

- Are there any values I'd like to focus on?

Once you've identified your values, you can create an affirmation. Identify that affirmation and work through the list of questions below.

To assess if your affirmation is believable, ask yourself:

- What would I like to believe?

- Does that belief feel possible? Can I imagine a world where that would be true?

- If it doesn't feel possible, how can I adjust the affirmation?

The affirmation needs to feel possible and have the potential to be true. This will vary depending on the person and their circumstances. What feels true for you might feel extremely unlikely for me. If I start with "I would like to love myself" and that doesn't actually feel possible, I might change the affirmation to "I will accept myself" or "I will try to love myself." Adding words like *possible*, *might*, or *try* can help an affirmation feel more flexible.

The affirmation also needs to be achievable. This means that you need to feel like you can make this affirmation come true through your own mental and physical efforts. Again, this is highly personal and what is achievable for me might not be possible for you. We are all different and interact with different supports and barriers in our lives. Try to avoid affirmations with absolutes like *always* or *never*, as they are even harder to achieve.

To assess if your affirmation is achievable, ask yourself:

- Does this feel realistic for me?

- Is this something that feels possible even if it's not realistic right now?

- Can I find the resources or support I need to make this happen?

- Is this affirmation flexible or does it use words like *always* or *never*?

It's OK to not have all the resources or tools to make your affirmation happen right now. What you want to focus on is how realistic this seems for you and if there is a possible path to get there. Many of us grow up hearing messages like "You can do anything you put your mind to" or "The only thing in the way is you." And while it's kind of a bummer that I have to say this, it's just not true. We have to look at what is achievable for our unique situation.

When I was a kid, I had to wear glasses so strong my eyes looked five times bigger behind the thick lenses. Without those glasses, I couldn't even identify my own mom. They didn't make contacts in my prescription at the time, so becoming number one on the swim team or playing a contact sport wasn't in the cards for me. Could I have done it if I had an escort to the pool and someone taught me how to dive in and swim without sight? Sure. But I would've spent so much time trying to develop a skill that wasn't really worth it. I would've missed out on cultivating all the other skills that were already within me. We all have different goals, talents, and abilities. If you're five feet four, securing a spot in the NBA probably isn't going to happen and that's OK. Those NBA players will never be gymnasts. It's all about finding what your skill set is and how to access the resources that will help you enhance it.

To decide how you will back up your affirmation with action, ask yourself:

- What would this affirmation look like in action?

- What will I do when living this affirmation feels hard?

- What will I do or what do I need to make this affirmation possible?

Most positive thinking literature ignores the power of action. Their methods are strictly focused on thought. Thoughts are powerful. Action is even more powerful. Once you have an affirmation, you need to live it or it will never be true. If you're constantly saying, "I love my body," but criticizing yourself at every turn and trying diet after diet, you're not going to feel like you love your body. This step is so important. I want you to try to identify one or two ways that you will live out this affirmation daily. How will you prove that this thought is true? It might feel forced or weird at first, but with repetition of thought and action it will become easier.

To make sure you're not using the affirmation to cover up for another distressing feeling, ask yourself:

- What is the purpose of this affirmation?

- Is this affirmation preventing me from processing another feeling?

- Does this affirmation help me process my emotions?

- Does this feel supportive or does it feel like denial?

Sometimes affirmations can be a little bit too positive. This is usually when I see things go wrong. These affirmations are being used to cover up something else—usually something bigger and more distressing. If you've just lost someone close to you and you're grieving, repeating "I love my life" every day isn't going to eliminate the grief. You will still have to go through it. If you're going through something really hard, it's best to have an affirmation that helps you move through that emotion. If I was grieving, I might say something like "This is hard and I will get through it" or "I am grieving and I am resilient." It helps to validate the real emotion you're feeling and add something that is empowering.

When we create an affirmation that is in line with our values, believable, achievable, backed up by action, and is supportive of our emotional experience, so much good can happen. The right affirmation can take us from hating something, to seeing a possibility for neutrality, into neutrality, and then into a place where the positive affirmation feels possible (maybe most or some of the time) and we're able to act out that affirmation through our thoughts and behaviors.

It's important to note that no affirmation is true every second of every day. You're never going to feel great about your body or any other part of your life all the time. The goal is acceptance, the ability to hold space for that fluctuation, and believing that being kind to yourself is allowed and helpful. As you practice this new way of developing affirmations, it will slowly become second nature and you will intuitively develop affirmations that support you and your current reality.

You Need to Feel Those Difficult Emotions

I open up my computer browser late one afternoon and Aly is already logged in for virtual therapy. She sits on the floor of her bedroom with homework and pens splayed out around her. She's young, but her insight far surpasses that of many of my adult clients. I find myself learning something from her in every session. Aly's relationship with her mother is chaotic. We spend most of our time focused on discussing boundaries and managing their most recent conflict.

Aly apologizes a lot in session. It's something she learned to do whenever her mother was upset. She apologizes for feeling, for not remembering something, for "burdening" me with her life. Whenever she apologizes, I jokingly say, "If you can't share your feelings here, where can you share them? It is literally my job to listen!" She laughs and nods. I reassure Aly that she doesn't have to worry about me or my feelings, but it's in her nature. She is always worried about someone or something, rarely attending to herself. Getting her to focus more on herself and less on others is a dance we often find ourselves doing.

Aly's chronic apologizing and deep levels of insight likely stem from her constant need to manage her mother's moods. Her mom can be erratic, demanding, and highly critical. As a child, Aly absorbed the blame for a lot of her mom's struggle and sought to always make things more peaceful at home. She has to stuff down all of her own distressing emotions because there literally isn't room for them. Her mom's moods fill the room and she can feel it.

Aly's mother is on one extreme end of the emotional expression spectrum—she feels fully and her feelings become everyone else's problem through her behavior. She doesn't know how to self-regulate. Because of this, Aly has learned to live on the other end of the spectrum. She's become a master at pretending, stuffing down emotions, and acting like everything is good all the time. Neither one of these extremes is helpful or manageable in the long term. We have to find a way to get Aly to the middle, even if her mother never changes. So, Aly and I begin working on helping her get in touch with and express those challenging emotions that she deems "negative."

There Are No Negative Emotions

Toxic positivity and the relentless pressure to use positive affirmations tells us that there are certain emotions we should feel, like happiness and joy, and others that we should absolutely avoid, like anger and disgust. There are thousands of books, videos, and websites dedicated to helping people eradicate all forms of emotional negativity from their lives. The goal is to reach this beautiful place where your thoughts are peaceful and joyous, your mind is clear, and nothing upsets you.

Spoiler alert: this place doesn't exist.

Emotions are an involuntary response to environmental stimuli and we don't have full control over our emotional experience. With proper skills training and a well-regulated nervous system, we can learn how to respond to our emotions and augment our behavior, but we will never have full control over what we feel. This type of behavioral control may be even more challenging for people who have experienced trauma, have a disorder that leads to nervous system dysregulation, or who do not have adequate skills to manage their emotions. You are never consciously saying to yourself, "Hmm, I think I'll get scared when that car slams on its brakes!" You are simply reacting.

Contrary to popular belief, there are no negative emotions. There are only emotions that are harder to experience or that cause more distress for certain people, and the more you suppress those emotions, the harder they are to manage. Some people may struggle more with joy or calm, while others avoid anger or anxiety. The feelings that we typically refer to as negative are sadness, anger, fear, and disgust. These tend to be emotions that we want to suppress or avoid because we don't like how they feel or how they make us behave. There's a reason these emotions are so difficult to manage. They make our brains release cortisol, the stress hormone. The prefrontal cortex then becomes unable to effectively process information. Our ability to learn or pay attention becomes significantly impaired and we struggle. But these emotions actually play a major role in our life and help protect us.

Difficult or distressing emotions like anger, fear, or disgust help you:

- Identify what is important

- Recognize when someone or something is upsetting

- Point to something that needs attention like a relationship or health issue

- Know when you're in danger

- Recognize when you need to rest or keep going

- Decide where you need a boundary or more flexibility

- Assess social situations

- Learn from mistakes

- Become more resilient

It's actually impossible to avoid these emotions and emotional distress altogether, and the more you try, the more distress you'll experience. Instead of learning how to get rid of challenging emotions, we need to learn how to sit with, process, and live with them.

Be Grateful, or Else

Gratitude is often something we use or are pressured to employ when we experience challenging emotions or complain. Everywhere you look there's someone or something telling you that you should be grateful for the roof over your head, the food on your plate, and even your traumas.

- "Be grateful it wasn't worse."

- "At least you have (insert whatever you should be grateful for)."

- "You have so much to be grateful for."

- "Someone with this much good in their life can't be depressed. Look on the bright side."

Gratitude, like happiness, has become a moral obligation that we must fulfill. Without it, our culture tells us, you're probably doomed to a life of sadness and loneliness. Every moment demands the presence of gratitude and it is exhausting.

People who are struggling really feel the pressure to be grateful. If you're anxious, it's because you're not focusing enough on the good. If you are grieving or dealing with loss, you need to remember what you have and focus less on what is gone. If you struggled to get pregnant, you can't complain about pregnancy or those late-night feeds. If you're struggling and you have a roof over your head and food on your table, you better get some perspective because others have it so much worse than you. And it's true, right? Someone else will always have it worse than you in one area and better than you in another. I think we can also agree that specific groups of people struggle more in key areas that really diminish their functioning and quality of life. Certainly things like poverty, food insecurity, unemployment, lack of education, and abuse or neglect are going to have a negative impact on people that often lasts a lifetime.

The problem with this logic is that we only know what we know. We're all living inside of our own orbits and if I tell someone struggling with an eating disorder, "Well, there are people starving around the world. Be grateful you have food and just eat something!" that is going to be incredibly stigmatizing and wildly unhelpful. It's way too hard for someone to draw a connection between those two realities when they're struggling. Plus, both things are true at the same time. This individual is battling an eating disorder and there are millions of children dealing with food insecurity around the world. One does not cancel out the suffering that is found in the other.

Gratitude, something that is supposed to make us aware of what we value and cherish in life, instead becomes a weapon of shame that we wield at ourselves and one another in our deepest moments of struggle. We use it to silence people and shut down conversations.

What if instead we made room for the bad and welcomed the good? Maybe then we could experience the true benefits of gratitude.

What Is Gratitude?

The concept of gratitude is easy to understand in theory, but often hard to put into practice. Gratitude is an overall orientation toward appreciating others and the world around us. We use this view to make decisions and create stories about our lives. Gratitude is believed to be a malleable trait that can be cultivated and improved throughout the life cycle. It's also a belief that can be challenged or strengthened depending on one's life circumstances and how they conceptualize those events.

The gratitude literature hasn't really tackled the prevalence of the gratitude trait across different demographics. What we do know is that gratitude has significant associations with age, gender, education level, and employment status. Older people, women, individuals with higher education, and employed individuals reported higher scores of the gratitude trait when compared to younger people, men, those with lower education levels, and unemployed individuals. These results show how the gratitude trait is not evenly distributed across populations and that we cannot apply the same strategies for every person. A recent study actually found that the grateful trait was a weak predictor of subjective well-being in the future when accounting for the effect of demographic factors. There are clearly cultural, gender, social, and personality differences when assessing gratitude levels among different populations. It is also evident that life experiences and access to certain resources have an impact on one's ability to show or experience gratitude.

Does Gratitude Work?

Gratitude lists, journals, reminders, and affirmations flood my Instagram feed daily. Usually these photos show a thin, white, ablebodied person in their perfectly curated kitchen. They tell me I need to be grateful no matter what or that "There's always something to be grateful for." That command stings when I'm struggling. There's something about being obligated to find the silver lining that just doesn't sit well with me.

Over the last ten years there has been a surge in research on gratitude and its potential impact on psychopathology, mental health, overall well-being, and physical health. Unfortunately, many of the benefits we are told gratitude has actually have quite limited evidence.

The relationship between gratitude and physical health has produced inconclusive results. Gratitude interventions appear to positively impact a number of cardiovascular and inflammatory markers and improve sleep quality. However, the effects of gratitude exercises on bodily functions do not differ from the effect of other distraction-type exercises. There is currently no convincing evidence to support a causal link between gratitude and reduced pain perception in chronically ill or chronic pain patients. Lastly, gratitude does not seem to directly predict physical health outcomes. I know this contradicts much of what I've been taught about gratitude. While I was working as a new therapist with patients diagnosed with cancer and their caregivers, gratitude interventions were the prescription of choice. It was widely accepted that an increase in gratitude could help someone recover physically at better rates than those who did not participate in a gratitude practice. You would be very likely to find a support group for cancer patients sharing what they're grateful for down the hall or a physician telling someone how important their attitude was if they wanted to recover.

Recent research does demonstrate that a regular gratitude practice moderately benefits mental well-being, emotional well-being, and social well-being. Evidence shows that gratitude interventions like journaling, when done regularly, do improve emotional well-being. This makes sense; gratitude allows us to orient our attention to what is good in our lives, and that often gives us a sense of control. If we focus solely on what we lack or what we don't have control over, it will only lead to feeling worse. The hard part is finding that balance and acknowledging both.

Gratitude unfortunately does not reduce symptoms of psychopathology or mental illness. Research suggests that positive psychology interventions are not always suitable for individuals with a history of mental illness, and their effectiveness is largely dependent on the resources an individual has available and the current adversity in their life. It may even be harmful to suggest gratitude as an initial form of treatment or coping when someone is dealing with mental illness or severe psychopathology. While cultivating a sense of gratitude has been suggested to aid in preventing mental health struggles following adversity, it should be used cautiously with individuals who are struggling with psychopathology. It's important to note that these tools are not one-size-fits-all and can be harmful when used as a substitute for formal mental health treatment, especially in more severe cases of mental illness.

Gratitude can be a powerful tool when used at the right time, by the right person, but we have to be cautious about applying it across all people and all situations.

I Know I Should Be Grateful, But . . .

Danny and I have been discussing his relationship with his mother. He is extremely introspective and quite hard on himself. As far as I know, his history doesn't include any major abuse or neglect. He describes his childhood as "normal." All assessments demonstrate that his mother was actually quite loving and she tried very hard to meet his needs, but Danny was a different kid than her other three children and she struggled immensely with relating to him. This meant his childhood was spent feeling quite isolated, misunderstood, and "different."

It has taken Danny about a year to come to terms with the fact that he can have issues with his childhood and even some negative feelings about his mother, while also being grateful for what he has. He starts off so many of his sentences with, "I know I should be grateful, but . . ." Then he goes on to share something like, "I had everything a kid could have ever wanted. I know so many other people had it worse. I feel bad even being here and talking about this." Danny compares himself to his friends who he knows experienced emotional or physical neglect as kids and is constantly using their experiences as a means to diminish his own. His gratitude is actually just leading to shame.

I know I've felt like Danny before; maybe you have, too. It's this feeling that I can't be upset or unhappy because I have so much to be grateful for. I use the phrase "I know so many people have it worse . . ." before uttering a complaint so that people understand that I'm not a complete monster; I'm just upset about this one little thing. Maybe I follow it up with, "But I'll get over it. I know I'm so lucky to even have this problem! Please don't judge me!" It's this never-ending cycle of feeling like you have to add the caveat of being grateful before expressing any type of discomfort.

You Can't Force Gratitude

Gratitude is important, and a little perspective never hurts. This is something that I often work on with my clients. We're always trying to find the gray area and make room for what hurts and what supports us. Acknowledging both gives us the room to grieve our losses and continue to function. If we constantly focused only on our lack or what we're missing, life would be impossibly dark and challenging. The problem arises when we try to force gratitude.

Forced gratitude looks something like this: You're having a really bad day. Your car broke down, you got stranded on the side of the road, and you missed an important meeting at work. Your boss is furious and you know that repairing your car is going to break the bank. This is very annoying, frustrating, and time-consuming. You call your mom to vent and maybe ask for some advice on where to get your car fixed. She responds by saying, "You should be so grateful you have a job and a car. Some people wish for these problems. It's all going to work out." You're still upset and in the thick of trying to figure out a solution to this problem, and gratitude is being forced upon you. Maybe you start to feel a hint of shame or regret. *She's right: many people don't have a car or a job. I should be grateful.* But this doesn't work because you are emotionally flooded, don't have a working vehicle, and your job may be in jeopardy. There is truth to this perspective but it's completely ineffective and guilt inducing.

Instead, we want to make space for the current feeling and then let the gratitude flow in, naturally. Let's continue with the broken-down car example to illustrate how you would do this.

1. Validate your current feelings: "It makes sense that I feel up-set. My car broke down and I disappointed my boss. My job

is really important to me and I don't have enough savings to fix my car right now."

2. If something needs to be fixed right now, focus on problem-solving: "I need to get off the side of the road and find a place to fix my car. I also need to communicate with my boss and figure out when I will be able to get back to work today."

3. Regulate your current emotions until you can get to a place of calm. When we're distressed, logical reasoning is challenging. Use some of your emotional regulation skills to help bring yourself back into the moment, clear your head, and get focused. This may take some time or several attempts.

4. Get some perspective. When your immediate concerns have been solved and you feel validated, you can engage in some perspective seeking and gratitude. This is when it might be helpful to look at what is going well in your life and what you have access to. This does not mean the other hard stuff doesn't exist; it's all happening at the same time. In this case I might say, "I'm so glad the tow truck was able to pick me up and I didn't get hurt. I'll be able to repair this with my boss because I am typically a reliable employee."

You may have to move through this cycle several times depending on the event or intensity of the feeling. It's absolutely normal to struggle with some of the stages or to get stuck.

How to Make Gratitude Work for You

There are so many ways to engage with gratitude throughout your day. Just remember, gratitude cannot exist without validation and emotional processing. Before you use any of these gratitude-enhancing skills, it's important to make sure that you're in a place where you're ready to receive and experience gratitude. If you move too quickly it will probably feel forced and unhelpful.

Here are some things you can do regularly to help improve your sense of gratitude:

- Hold space for both the good and the bad in your life by paying attention to and recognizing both. It usually helps to start with the parts you're struggling with most and then go for gratitude.

- Write about the things that you are grateful for. You can journal about a particular topic, make a list, draw a picture, or do anything that orients your attention to the feeling of gratitude.

- Say thank you and acknowledge people. It feels really good to help others and this also improves our social bonds. Make it a point to say thank you, smile, and compliment others.

The most important component of cultivating gratitude is doing it regularly and not just in moments of intense struggle. The more you're able to validate your feelings, solve problems effectively, and develop perspective, the more likely you are to develop a consistent state of gratitude.

Just remember, problems are always relative. There will always be someone who has it worse than you; there will always be someone who has it better. That's not going to stop you from feeling. We can make room for validation and gratitude at the same time. Validation says, "This is hard and I know it could be better." Gratitude is: "I'm grateful for what I have. I know others have it worse. I know it could be worse." Other people having it worse or things being "not that big of a deal" isn't going to change how it feels. The trick is balancing the two.

We can make room for validation and gratitude at the same time.

Here's an example of validation paired with gratitude: "What I'm going through right now is hard and frustrating. I give myself permission to recognize that. After I validate myself, I'll turn to gratitude. I know I have a lot to be grateful for, but someone else's struggle being greater doesn't lessen mine."

You may benefit from creating your own gratitude statement that validates what you're feeling and makes room for the possibility that things could get better.

Reflection

Take a moment to think about gratitude. Answer the following questions honestly and openly.

- When did you first learn that you should be grateful? What beliefs were you taught about gratitude?

- Do you ever feel pressured to display gratitude?

- How can you incorporate gratitude into your life in a way that makes sense and helps you feel better?

Your thoughts create your reality.

....

Your thoughts are powerful but they don't create your entire reality. You are a dynamic human being who is influenced by so many different people, places, things, and systems. We can create systemic change and empower people to use their thoughts to inspire and motivate.

. . . .

Chapter Five

How to Process an Emotion

Alissa's work schedule has been chaotic, so she's cut back to one session a month. Like most infrequent therapy, we spend the first half of the session catching up. She's lonely, overworked, exhausted, and wearing an emotional armor so thick I can barely pierce through. "I'm doing OK. I'll get through it," she whispers. Her voice is low and weak. Alissa and I are always doing this dance. She comes to therapy, tells me she's fine. I stare back at her sullen eyes and gray complexion, knowing full well that she's not telling me or herself the truth. Alissa isn't allowing herself to feel anything, and all the numbing with work and moving at a frenetic pace won't stop the emotions from seeping through. Her feelings are going to show up, whether she likes it or not.

I decide to push a little and ask Alissa what's really going on: "Is this just about work or is there something I'm missing here?"

She stares down at the floor, pondering her next move, and I sit there quietly, hoping my suspicion cracks her armor slightly. Alissa tells me that all her friends are getting married, having babies, and "moving on." She feels stuck and lost. "My work is killing me and it's all I have." A single tear falls from her face and she wipes it away quickly.

I decide to prompt her again: "Are you feeling any of this? You seem a little numb to it all. I'm not sure I could manage keeping this all under wraps if it were me." I can tell she's stuck and has absolutely no idea where to go from here. I try to stay quiet and let her process my question. She looks up at me and says, "I honestly have no idea how I would even feel this. What does that even mean?" Her frustration is palpable, and it's typical of people who have been suppressing and running from their emotions for a long time. They have no idea how to feel an emotion and denial seems like the only option. I want to try to show Alissa a way out of this loop and how to feel her emotions.

What Is an Emotion?

Emotions are something that all humans experience, but we don't all experience them in the same way. Many people use the terms "feeling" and "emotion" interchangeably; they're not the same thing.

- An emotion is a physiological experience (like a rapid heartbeat or difficulty breathing) that gives you information about the world. It's a complex reaction pattern that is determined by the significance of the event.

- A feeling is your conscious awareness of the emotion itself.

Feelings are experienced consciously, while emotions manifest either consciously or subconsciously. With emotional education and practice, some people are able to experience an emotion and give it a name or a label, making it a feeling that they're able to understand and experience. This is a skill that is taught and learned; you're not born knowing how to do this, and there are a wide variety of emotional experiences depending on the individual. Many people, like Alissa, really struggle with this. Alissa is experiencing emotions but she isn't feeling them. The denial and suppression of her emotional experience makes it extremely difficult for her to understand the feeling. This is a common experience for people who are unaware of their emotions, what emotions feel like in the body, and how they manifest. For them, the emotion and how they're experiencing it are not connected. This means that they may have to experience this emotion continuously for a long period of time before they recognize its presence. Letting emotions go on like this can lead to negative consequences both physically and mentally.

How We Form Emotions

Emotions were originally viewed as a trivial part of human life, not worthy of study or investigation. Charles Darwin did recognize that emotions had some utility and were critical for our survival and adaptability, but not much else was gleaned from this realization. In the 1990s, psychologists Peter Salovey and John Mayer introduced the first formal theory of emotional intelligence. They defined it as "the ability to monitor one's own and others' feelings and emotions, to discriminate among them and to use this information to guide one's thinking and actions."

Today, there are several prominent theories about how emotions work. I like the theory developed by Lisa Feldman Barrett. In her book *How Emotions Are Made*, Dr. Barrett explains that emotions are not built in at birth; they're something that we develop throughout our life, and how we feel and show our emotions largely depends on our unique experiences. These experiences allow the brain to become a "predictive learning machine." We take in new experiences and compare them to our past ones. The emotions that we feel in the moment are instantaneous meanings that the brain is giving to these internal and external sensory experiences. Dr. Barrett explains that "emotions are your brain's best guess of how you should feel in the moment. Emotions aren't wired into your brain like little circuits; they're made on demand." This is all happening unconsciously and largely without our knowledge. This means our emotions are created in the moment based on sensory input from our body and our surroundings, our goals, and memories from our prior experiences.

If we have a lot of negative experiences growing up, live in an environment that is scary and unreliable, or don't know what certain emotions or bodily sensations mean, it's likely that our predictions will land us in a lot of trouble. We have to learn how to interpret and manage our emotions as we age. Alissa's experiences have led her to interpret emotions in certain ways. This also impacts how she behaves when she experiences certain emotions and shows why she is so prone to denial and suppression. Emotions will have a major impact on our inner and outer worlds if we don't know how to interpret, process, and manage them.

How Emotions Work

We know that three things happen when we experience an emotion: the body and brain change, our thoughts change, and we respond to the emotion through action or behavior. Emotions are not just thoughts in the mind; they also produce real changes in the body. When you have an emotional reaction, the brain changes what's happening in the body. If you are afraid or angry, you might feel your heart beat faster or your breathing might speed up. When you're feeling sad, you might get tears in your eyes. Emotions can also cause some muscles in your body to move automatically or prepare you for movement. A lot of what is happening in the body is completely unconscious and you may not even know you're doing it. The body may also react before the mind, leading you to interpret the emotion based on what is happening in your body. If you feel your heart racing, you might think it's excitement or anxiety. If you feel your stomach churning and your head feels clouded, you might interpret this as fear or confusion.

When you experience an emotion, you may notice that your thoughts often change to match that emotion. Thoughts can also cause emotions to develop or intensify. For example, if you start to notice that your heart is beating faster and it's hard to breathe, you might begin to have anxious thoughts like *I'm not safe here* or *I need to get out of here.* If you're lying in bed thinking about something that makes you anxious, it's expected that your body will start to react as if it's experiencing the real threat at that moment. This is because the brain isn't able to fully differentiate between a real threat and one that is imagined. You can induce panic with your thoughts.

Emotions end up having the biggest impact through our behavior. Our most primitive emotions, like fear, were designed to keep us alive and safe. If you're being chased by a bear, your heart starts beating faster, adrenaline courses through your veins, and you are pushed to act, often by running away. This type of emotional reaction is essential for our survival. Fortunately, the world has changed immensely since we were regularly chased by bears, but our brains have not. This means that we may behave in ways that are totally hyper- or underreactive depending on the level of threat. Someone with social anxiety may experience a sensation of being judged. Their body tenses up, it feels like everyone is staring at them, and they start thinking *I need to get out of here!* The sensations in the body, paired with their anxious thoughts, lead them to run out of the room and to avoid social situations for the next few months. Were they really under threat? Would they have died if they stayed in the room? Probably not, but it felt like they would have and that is why they acted this way. This is why it's so important to develop an understanding of our emotions and to develop the tools to deal with them.

The Risks of Not Labeling, Experiencing, and Sharing Our Emotions

Emotional suppression is an emotion regulation strategy that we use in an attempt to make uncomfortable, overwhelming thoughts and feelings more manageable or go away completely. It's a strategy that many people learned in childhood and continue to use as adults. In moderation, emotional suppression can actually be useful or neutral. But when we do it too often, it can become detrimental to our physical and mental health.

You may attempt to suppress your emotions or dismiss them in a lot of different ways. Here are some common ways we suppress emotions:

- eating and drinking

- using drugs or alcohol

- distracting yourself through TV, work, or other means

- traveling

- socializing and constantly surrounding yourself with people

- exercising

- helping others

- using positive sayings or other types of self-help and self-improvement

In many situations, these are actually good or neutral coping mechanisms. You don't need to stop completely or label them as bad. The problem arises when we consistently use these coping skills to avoid, suppress, and deny the existence of a feeling. It inevitably intensifies emotional distress.

Some of the ways we numb and distract ourselves are more socially acceptable than others. When someone says, "I am just so busy with work! I don't have any time for my marriage or my children," we're more apt to forgive and rationalize. We think, *They're working so hard! The family benefits from their hard work. It's OK.* But when someone is numbing or avoiding emotions through sex or drugs, the judgment flies.

Avoidance usually leads us to the same place—no matter how we decide to avoid.

Distress, discomfort, and anxiety are all a guaranteed part of life. Emotional avoidance is often only a temporary and superficial solution. This avoidance reinforces the idea that experiences like discomfort, distress, and anxiety are bad or dangerous. It reduces your ability to face and tolerate necessary pain. Suppression also requires a lot of energy and often leaves you feeling exhausted as it begins to take more and more effort to cover up the difficult emotion.

Avoidance is not the same as distraction. Many distraction techniques have proven to be useful in the moment and allow for greater emotional processing. Avoidance is devoid of acceptance. It is a quest to numb, eliminate, and deny that the feeling is even happening. Emotional avoidance often doesn't work. When you tell yourself not to think about something, you have to think about not thinking about it. When you try to avoid an emotion, you often end up feeling it anyway. And usually it's ten times worse.

There are also some real physical and mental consequences for emotional suppression over time, such as:

- more thoughts about the topic you're trying to push away

- increased risk for anxiety and depression symptoms

- muscle tension and pain

- nausea and digestive problems

- appetite changes

- fatigue and sleep problems

- high blood pressure

- digestive problems

- cardiovascular disease

- feeling numb or blank

- feeling nervous, low, or stressed a lot of the time and not understanding why

- a tendency to forget things

- unease or discomfort when other people talk about their feelings

- feeling distressed or irritated when someone asks you about your feelings

Before you start labeling, feeling, and sharing your emotions, it's important to investigate what emotions you tend to want to suppress and how you are suppressing them.

- First, identify one or two difficult emotions that tend to pop up in your life.

- What strategies do you typically use to avoid this emotion?

- There are always advantages (pros) for avoidance. Write down a couple of reasons why this avoidance feels good or helps. It's important to validate that there is often a short-lived, positive effect from emotional avoidance.

- Now write down any cons of this emotional avoidance. Has it caused any pain, suffering, or other issues in your life?

Instead of suppressing your emotions, you can work on the more adaptive skills of labeling, feeling, and sharing your emotions with others.

Labeling Your Emotions

Simply knowing what emotion you're experiencing and being able to give it a label can transform your emotional experience and help you feel more at ease. Psychologist Matthew Lieberman conducted a study using functional magnetic resonance imaging (fMRI) to scan the brains of participants. The researchers found that when the participants labeled the emotions they felt using words, they showed less activity in the amygdala—an area of the brain associated with emotional distress. They proposed that verbalizing an emotion and labeling it suppresses the area of the brain that produces emotional pain.

This method has also been shown to be effective in therapy. I've been doing this in session with Alissa. First, we investigate what is going on in her body. This will help her tap into her emotional experience and how her body and mind are interpreting the world. We spend a lot of time here because this is new for her. She feels calm in session, but notes that her chest usually feels tight at work, especially when she is around certain coworkers. You can walk yourself through the same process that I used with Alissa by using the questions below. If you're a trauma survivor or have ever struggled with dissociation or flashbacks, it's best to walk through this with a trusted professional or companion.

1. Take a moment to sit with your body. You can lie down or sit comfortably. Find a way to make yourself feel grounded. It may help to have your back against something firm like a wall or a chair and have your feet planted firmly on the ground.

2. With your eyes open or closed—again, whatever feels safest and most comfortable for you—start to scan your body from the top of your head to the bottom of your feet. Take a moment to notice any sensations that are popping up for you.

3. When you notice a spot where there is tension or a sense of relaxation, don't do anything about it. Just notice it. No judgment, no questions, no analysis.

4. Is there a spot in your body where the sensation is more intense? Can you go to that spot and really examine it? What sensations are you experiencing? Is it getting less or more intense?

5. Now take a moment to ground yourself in the present moment. Look around at your surroundings and ground yourself in your body. You've just completed your body check-in.

This exercise will help you check in with your body and learn more about what it feels like to experience those sensations. If you're like Alissa and have been numbing out or really disconnected, you might not feel anything the first time you do this. That's OK, keep practicing.

After we practiced checking in with the sensations in the body, Alissa and I started working on labeling the emotions. Here are some of the questions I asked her:

1. If you could give this emotion a name, what would it be?

2. If this sensation in your body could talk, what do you think it would say?

3. Does this feel like something you have felt before? If yes, what did you call it then?

4. How would you describe this feeling?

5. Let's try it out. When you say "I feel _____," does that seem right?

6. When you choose a feeling word, say "I feel _____." Try to avoid saying "I am (the feeling)."

There are more than four thousand feeling words to describe our emotional state. Here are some commonly used words:

Happy	Lonely	Worried
Loved	Disappointed	Anxious
Relieved	Hopeless	Doubtful
Contented	Unhappy	Annoyed
Amused	Lost	Stressed

How to Feel Your Emotions and Feelings

In my next session with Alissa, we reviewed how to look for sensations in her body and to label feelings. She said she's becoming more aware of her bodily sensations, but is still struggling with labeling them: "I just don't get how I'm supposed to feel something. It doesn't make any sense to me." I reassure her that this is common and it's something I struggle with, too. Today we will start learning how to actually feel emotions and what that looks like.

Alissa knows that her emotions are forming in two major ways:

- Her body is reacting through physical sensations. She is then taking in those sensations (usually subconsciously), interpreting them, and creating a story in her mind via her thoughts.

- She is thinking about something or taking in stimuli from her environment. Her body is reacting to these thoughts and helping to create her overall emotional experience.

This is the cycle that many of us experience. The body and the mind are working together to create our own personal emotional experience. Our thoughts and physical sensations are helping us identify exactly what we're feeling, and this dictates what we are going to do with that information. If you want more control over your behaviors, you really need to feel the emotion and let it move through you. If you react too quickly, you will probably misinterpret the emotion or say something you don't actually mean. If you wait too long, you run the risk of suppressing your emotions or even getting hurt physically or emotionally. So, after the noticing, recognizing, and labeling comes the feeling.

When we talk about "feeling" our feelings, what we're really saying is that you have to allow yourself to experience the full breadth of the emotion and allow it to rise, peak, and then fall. You have to allow your body to complete the stress cycle and decide how you'd like to deal with this feeling or emotion. There are many ways to actually experience your feelings and emotions; most of them are not calculated, intellectual decisions. They also have to happen in the body.

The next time you're noticing an emotion in your body, try following the questions that I used with Alissa. Then attempt to label the feeling and give it a name. Now comes the hard part: you're not going to numb that feeling or run from it. Instead, you're going to experience it. Following is a list of ways to experience that emotion.

- Move: Go for a walk, stretch, move your body in a way that feels right for you.

- Breathe: Deep, slow breaths help regulate the stress response. You might want to use an app on your phone or practice this with your therapist.

- Connect: Get out in public around people and have casual, positive interactions. Even just smiling at the barista making your coffee and saying "Thank you" helps.

- Laugh: This helps create and maintain social bonds and regulate emotions. You can laugh with friends or watch a funny video to help you laugh.

- Touch: Hug or kiss someone who you like and trust. You can also wrap your arms around your chest to give yourself a hug. Safe physical touch helps regulate the nervous system.

- Journal: Writing about your feelings has been shown to help people manage their emotions, process them, and make better decisions.

- Cry: A tried-and-true method that really works and has cathartic effects for us mentally and physically.

- Talk it out: Processing something emotionally with a trusted person or professional can be really helpful and allows you to tap into that labeling skill. This may also help with decision making and safe emotional processing.

- Express yourself creatively: Art, writing a poem, or using your hands to create can be extremely helpful for processing emotions.

- Complete a task: Getting into a flow state while cooking, cleaning, gardening, or doing something with your hands can create a sense of accomplishment and help you eliminate some racing thoughts.

- Listen to music: Music has been shown to elevate your mood and motivation and reduce stress. Listen to something inspiring, calming, or that elicits an emotion you're trying to experience.

- Sleep: When used correctly, this can be a great way to process an emotion. Sleeping and then attending to an emotion can be an effective way to cool down.

- Just feel it: This is a skill that may take some time, but it's very helpful. Sometimes the feeling doesn't mean anything and you don't need to act. So you just sit with it and allow it to peak, then slowly pass. The more often you're able to do this, the easier it will be for feelings to not compound and become overwhelming.

Sometimes you have to postpone feeling a feeling because you're at work or dealing with your kids. Not every feeling can be felt fully in the moment and that's OK. What is important is that you're factoring in moments throughout your week to attend to your emotions and really experience them. The more you do this, the easier it will become. You may even start feeling your emotions and processing them without planning for it in a conscious way.

How to Share Your Emotions and Feelings

Feeling our feelings is helpful, but we also benefit immensely from sharing them with others. Humans are social beings and connecting through an emotional experience allows us to form social bonds, process our feelings, and ultimately feel better. Expressing feelings is a challenge for many people for a variety of reasons. Maybe you were never taught how to feel an emotion, or when you did express yourself, you were shamed or ignored. We don't come out of the womb knowing how to feel, label, and express our emotions, and there are a variety of gender and cultural norms that dictate expression within communities. What is "normal" for me may not be "normal" for you, and that's OK.

When we refer to how someone expresses their feelings, we're talking about their affect. *Affect* is someone's external expression of their internal emotional experience. For most people, there is congruence between affect and circumstance. For example, if you were told that your pet passed away, the expected reaction would be tears or some form of grief. For a percentage of the population, their external expression of emotion may not make sense or be the standard expression for the majority of people. Their outward emotional expression may also be totally incongruent with what they're feeling internally.

Our ability to express and regulate our emotions can be changed or impacted by our experiences, especially during childhood. Certain physical, neurological, and mental health conditions can also impede emotional expression or make communicating feelings in a "socially acceptable manner" even more difficult. People who have a brain tumor, brain damage, dementia, a brain injury, or head trauma may also have significant trouble with managing and expressing emotions because of structural damage to important parts of the brain. Mental health diagnoses like depression, schizophrenia, bipolar disorder, schizoaffective disorder, and post-traumatic stress disorder can also lead to inappropriate affect. These individuals usually haven't lost the ability to experience emotions; instead they have lost the ability to have them occur in a normal and expected way. This may be due to delusions, hallucinations, or faulty thought patterns and can often be treated through medication or behavioral interventions.

If you've struggled with your emotional expression, remember that you have to learn how to feel and express your emotions, and sometimes we don't have the best teachers. There are also a variety of ways to experience and express emotions. You have to find the way that works for you and that might not always be what is considered "normal" in your culture or where you live. There isn't anything wrong with you if you're struggling with this, and sometimes we have to teach ourselves and the people we love how we express our emotions.

Toxic positivity has a large impact on our ability to connect emotionally. We're afraid to share how we're feeling because we'll appear "negative" or "ungrateful." The pressure to have it all and do it all keeps us trapped in beautifully decorated cages. We don't have to share everything with everyone, and you are allowed to maintain privacy in your life. But when we only share the good and keep all of the struggle hidden, shame is sure to arise. If you grew up being told to keep your emotions to yourself or that anything negative should be concealed, you may have learned that showing emotions would just get you into more trouble, so you kept everything inside because it was easier that way. You learned that independence is a virtue and needing people is a weakness. I see this in my office all the time. I know so many high-achieving people who still feel empty. On the outside they're thriving, and on the inside they don't know how to get their needs met. They don't know how to connect or share; they don't even know they're allowed to. Remember that your need for attention and connection is primal. There is no medal or award for handling everything yourself. There's no trophy for being the most independent or the "strongest." You're not weak because you need people and you need support. It's OK to express your emotions; it's what makes you human.

It's OK to express your emotions; it's what makes you human.

Ways to Share Your Emotions with Others

You don't have to share your emotions with everyone, and there are certain people and environments that aren't conducive to productive emotional sharing. Some people do not have the skills to help you through a difficult time. I want you to always remember, no one has a right to your story. You are allowed to share as much or as little as you want. There are also certain people who might feel safer for specific topics and others who do not.

Here are some guidelines for sharing your emotions with others.

Pick a safe person to share with. Signs of a safe person:

- I can share my feelings without fear of the relationship ending or punishment.

- This person respects my boundaries.

- This person encourages me to grow, change, and better myself.

- This person respects my boundaries around my body and physical touch.

- I can usually be vulnerable around this person.

- This person admits when they are wrong and is open to feedback.

- This person refrains from using criticism and contempt to attack me or make me feel less than.

- This person listens to me.

- This person has the bandwidth and experience to help me through this issue.

- I feel comfortable discussing this topic with this person.

You also have the right to develop a relationship before sharing, and you are not required to share with everyone—even if they ask or push you. Excessive vulnerability that leaves you feeling exposed and unsupported is not the antidote to toxic positivity. What's important is that you share on your terms with the right people. If you are supporting someone, it is also OK to say "I really want to support you, but I don't feel able to at this time." You can create safety and bonds in another way until your relationship becomes stronger.

Pick the right time and place.
Consider your environment before sharing. Think about where you are and if it is a safe space for you and the person receiving the information. Loud or crowded spaces may suddenly feel unsafe. Evaluate your surroundings and check in with yourself often. It's also OK to take your time. You are not required to finish a story or move quickly.

Respect boundaries.
Remember to respect your own boundaries and the boundaries of others. We never know what someone else has been through and how they will receive certain information.

Avoid adding these dismissive words or phrases when sharing about your emotions.

- "Lol"

- "It's not a big deal, but . . ."

- "Ha-ha"

- "It's whatever"

- "I don't care"

- "It's all good, but . . ."

- "You probably don't care, but . . ."

- "Never mind"

Communicate what you need from the other person.

- "I really need to vent right now."

- "I'm looking for some advice. Can you help me?"

- "I honestly just need someone to listen. It's been a rough week."

It would be nice if people always knew what we wanted, but they usually don't. Try to help them out with what your expectations are, how they can be helpful, and what you need from this emotional share.

Remember that the other person's reaction does not invalidate your emotional experience.
If they dismiss you, ignore your needs, or aren't validating, it's OK. This doesn't mean you did something wrong. You may need to choose another person to share with or speak with a therapist. Don't let this stop you from sharing.

Emotional Expression That Works for You

Using these tools to help you feel and express your emotions will improve your mental health. However, we have to be careful and find that perfect balance between too much emotional expression and too little. We know that not expressing your emotions, especially for long periods of time, can lead to dissociation, chronic pain or disease, the inability to communicate effectively, difficulty forming relationships, insomnia, and intrusive thoughts. This is why it's so important to learn how to identify your emotions, label your feelings, and express them in a healthy way.

Unfortunately, too much emotional expression can also have a negative impact on our lives. If you're always crying at work or posting about every feeling on the internet, there are probably going to be some difficult consequences. We talked earlier about how there are different expectations within cultures, genders, and certain situations for emotional expression. For example, you may be able to freely express your emotions at home with your spouse, but you need to be able to keep them under wraps during that important work meeting. There is no standard amount of emotional expression that is acceptable across all people, places, and situations. What's important is that you find the right amount of emotional expression and types of emotional expression that work for you.

Take a moment to think about:

- Which people in my life can I safely share my emotions with?

- Which areas in my life require me to alter or hide parts of my emotional experience?

- In which areas in my life do I feel comfortable sharing my full emotional experience?

- Are there any cultural norms that might impact how comfortable I am expressing my emotions? Do I want to integrate these norms into my life?

- Are there any gender norms that might impact how comfortable I am expressing my emotions?

- Are there certain people or places that make it harder for me to express my emotions?

You can use the answers to these questions to help you decide where and when are safe and productive places to share and express your emotions. The goal of emotional expression is to feel more understood and supported, not to feel worse. This means that choosing when, where, and with whom we share our emotions is extremely important.

When you love what you have, you have everything you need.

. . . .

You don't have to love every part of your life, and even when you do, you still might need more or want more. You do not have to accept less or being treated poorly in the name of gratitude. Allow yourself to be grateful for what is and hopeful for what could be.

Chapter Six

How to Complain Effectively

Complaining has a really bad reputation. Articles and gurus insist that too much complaining will "lower your vibration" and stop you from achieving your dreams, having friends, and living the life you want. They suggest that you cut out negativity from your life, especially people who complain.

Complaining is something we all do despite our best efforts to quit the so-called bad habit. This is because it is one of the main ways that we bond with others and create emotional connection. It's an effective way to share how you feel, connect, and evoke empathy in the listener. Complaints are how we let people know what we need and how to meet our needs. It also gives us a peek at what is important and what might be bothering us a little too much.

We know that excessive emotional suppression and eliminating all complaining from your life will have a negative effect on your health and well-being. Similarly, too much complaining isn't good for you and will have negative consequences. It's all about finding the balance and complaining effectively.

Take a moment to think about your relationship with complaining:

- Do you feel comfortable sharing complaints?

- How do you feel after complaining?

- What messages did you receive about complaining growing up?

- How do you feel when others are complaining?

We each have a unique relationship with the act of complaining, shaped by our personality, gender, cultural norms, and what we were exposed to. There are also a variety of topics that are seen as acceptable complaints and others that people find inappropriate or bothersome. Each person has their own threshold for complaining. You may notice that you can empathize or listen to someone up to a certain point, but when you're done, you're done.

What Is Complaining and Why Do We Do It?

Complaining by definition is the expression of dissatisfaction or annoyance about something. It's not inherently a bad thing. We are always going to be dissatisfied and annoyed with certain aspects of life, and talking about it does have some utility.

Humans love to complain. I know this because I get paid to sit with people while they vent, complain, and process every week. "Having a place to vent" is actually one of the most common reasons people ask to work with me. It's one of the reasons Sam comes to sit on my couch every week. I think most would describe what he does as complaining; I see it as a lens into his needs and what is important to him.

Sam talks about his business partner, his wife, his financial situation, and his kids. Even though he tends to skew more negative in session, he's grateful, self-reflective, and takes responsibility for his actions when needed. Sam loves to share and seeks validation. The sharing typically seems cathartic for him, but sometimes I wonder if he's complaining a little too much and that our therapy is becoming much more of a venting hour rather than treatment focused on a specific change-oriented goal. Sometimes I hear this voice in the back of my head that says, "Come on, Whitney, intervene. He needs to change. Give him a suggestion. Interrupt this litany of complaints." Occasionally I give in to the voice. I regret it every single time.

Recently I intervened while Sam was lamenting about the way his wife sorts the laundry. I could tell he was taken aback when I paused and asked him if this complaining was helpful and tried to redirect the conversation toward setting boundaries with his partner. Sam looked up at me like he hadn't fully finished his thought. His mouth was open and he seemed either confused or annoyed. I'm not sure. But what I do know is that I cut him off in the middle of his processing; all he wanted me to do right then was listen. Sam was not ready for my suggestions and, frankly, he never asked me for any advice. In later sessions we got into why Sam seems to seek out validation in therapy and where else he may not be getting it at home. We also talked about finding validation in spaces outside of therapy, including self-validation. There is therapeutic value in his venting and complaining. I made a note in my notebook to ignore the voice in my head that tells me to prematurely interject and assured myself that there is always something productive to be found in the therapeutic process if I allow it to flow naturally.

We've all been Sam. Everywhere you look, someone is complaining about the construction on the highway that isn't finished yet, their annoying boss, and the guy who cut them off in traffic. We even complain about our friend who won't stop complaining. Are we complaining too much? Maybe. Are we not complaining effectively? Probably. But let's be honest, complaining is an ancient human form of catharsis and connection, and it's never going away.

Is Complaining Bad for You?

Like anything, too much complaining can negatively impact your mental and physical well-being. Recurring negative thoughts do often lead to more negative thoughts. Excessive complaining can also cause you to release more of the stress hormone cortisol. Elevated levels of cortisol have been shown to interfere with memory and learning, lower immune function, and increase blood pressure and cholesterol. Excessive complaining and ruminating may also keep you stuck on a problem and make it hard to form social connections. One of the most common consequences of excessive complaining is a negative impact on your relationships because, well, it can get annoying. We may love to complain, but listening to a lot of complaining can also become challenging.

The amount of complaining that would be deemed excessive is highly individualized and depends on things like temperament, personality, life experience, and genetics. For example, the personality trait of agreeableness is associated with less complaining. Extroverts are also more sensitive to subtle nuances in social encounters, meaning they may recognize when there is a threat of social disapproval for complaining and stop before that threshold is reached. Even when they are highly dissatisfied, extroverts may be less likely to complain in order to maintain social bonds and social approval.

The best way to tell if your complaining is excessive is by looking at how it's impacting your life. Excessive complaining will eventually feel bad and keep you stuck. It doesn't liberate you, connect you to others, or make you feel relief. Instead, it leaves you feeling trapped. We know that excessive complaining isn't great for our health, and we know that suppressing emotions and trying to be positive all the time isn't, either. The right amount of complaining will show you what is important, create change in the world, help you get important feedback from others, and effectively process your emotions.

Why We Complain

Most of my clients will preface their complaining with, "I know I shouldn't complain but . . ." I'm quick to ask them, "Where did you learn that you shouldn't complain?" If there's a desire to share about an experience and its impact on you, but you feel a sense of shame or guilt for having that need, I think that is something worth exploring. Complaining does serve a real purpose in our lives, and once we discover how to effectively integrate it, great things can happen.

Complaining does serve a real purpose in our lives.

Complaints are typically used for two purposes: to change someone else's behavior and to make ourselves feel better. One of the main reasons we complain is catharsis—to vent our frustrations. Research has found that infrequent complainers who were asked to write about their dissatisfaction with a problem felt better when they were able to write about their complaints compared to writing about innocuous events from the previous day. Attempting to suppress emotions usually leads people to ruminate or make the problem even bigger than it is, illustrating how valuable this sharing and acknowledging of complaints can be. This type of exercise also gives the issues a container. You sit down, look at what is bothering you, get it on paper, and then can eventually walk away and leave it there. With bigger issues you may need a stronger intervention, but simple journal writing tends to be really effective for those smaller complaints.

Not all complaining is about being dissatisfied. We also complain to influence how other people feel about us. You probably have a friend who complains about the quality of the wine at a restaurant to show how superior their taste is. Or maybe they talk about how disgusting the hotel rooms were on a recent vacation. It was so bad that they'll never stay there again! This is a classic way of using complaining to create an impression of superiority or to make us feel better about ourselves. By complaining about something "bad," we're demonstrating authority, establishing our status, and aligning ourselves with what is "good." This type of complaining is used to identify yourself as a certain type of person and to create belonging within a group. Look out for this in your conversations. I bet you'll see it often.

We also use complaints as an entry point to discuss positive events. I do this all the time and I notice so many of my clients do, too. As I'm writing this book, I find myself complaining about the work as a way to discuss the book. It's common that people will complain about positive events like weddings or pregnancy by discussing the stress or negative symptoms. It makes sense: we really want to share about this exciting milestone and often we feel that sharing will be seen as boastful or arrogant. By sharing, "Gosh, this wedding is costing so much. I can't believe the price of the food!" we're giving ourselves the opportunity to discuss something that's important to us and create social bonds around the topic.

We use complaining as a way to get information from others and assess their opinions about certain issues. If you complain about your boss around your coworkers, you might be hoping to assess how they feel about the boss and identify if you have any allies or enemies around the office. You're sharing a complaint as a way to build alliances and figure out who is on your team. This also allows you to assess what types of opinions and complaints you can express in the future that will be validated, supported, and shared by the group. This type of complaining may help us form social connections and feel seen, heard, and accepted by the people who share our complaints.

Our desire for sympathy and attention is another major reason we complain. Think about the things you complain about. What are you looking for when you share? I would bet that a lot of the time it's validation like, "Yeah, that is annoying," or maybe you want some actual physical assistance from someone. Complaining alerts others that we're in need and lets them know how they can support us. It's our way of saying, "Hey! Look at me! I really need some help here." It helps people recognize that we are in pain and illustrates what we're struggling with. If you never complained or shared what was bothering you, it would be impossible for people to know that you needed help. I think this type of complaining is one of the most important types because it is the way we access social support within our communities and how we can access empathy for others.

Perhaps one of the most important reasons we complain is to hold people accountable for their behavior. On a small scale, you might do this when a restaurant gets your order wrong, or on a larger scale, when we hold our government accountable for unmet promises. If we want something to change, we have to make our complaints known. This type of sharing is often dismissed as "negativity." We have to remember that most major social justice movements in history began with a complaint. Someone noticed that something wasn't right, pointed it out, and had the courage to speak out about that injustice. These types of complaints are often met with the most resistance because they force us to look at ourselves, admit when we are wrong, and take on some really challenging and necessary work. We absolutely need this type of complaining if there's going to be any real change in the world.

Complaining helps us feel better, influences how people see us, creates social bonds, allows us to gather information, encourages empathy, and helps create real change. It plays a very important role in our lives and is a skill that when used correctly can be extremely effective.

Why Complaining Bothers Us

Complaining can bring out some pretty complicated emotions because it forces us to face real issues in the world and it often makes us feel helpless. We may want to silence the person talking about a social justice issue that's important to them because it bums us out and makes us have to acknowledge our own privilege. We want to skip that talk about our friend's health because it makes us face our own mortality or our inability to help. We don't want to take the time to listen to someone share about what's annoying them because we just have too much on our own plate. Listening to someone else complaining is usually one of the easiest ways to get uncomfortable, especially if we don't understand why the person is complaining or what they're looking for from us.

There are specific types of complaints that tend to be more bothersome than others. One of the more annoying types is what psychiatrist Eric Berne calls the "help-rejecting complainer." They share a problem and then receive a suggestion on how to solve it. The complainer then says, "Yes, but . . ." and continues to reject any of the proposed solutions. I've worked with so many clients who are stuck in this pattern. Early on in my career I would keep searching for the right intervention that would be accepted by the client. The issue is, problem-solving isn't the objective for this complainer. They may actually just want sympathy and attention, but the other person is clearly under the impression that they're looking for help.

So they keep offering suggestion after suggestion until one or both of them gets intensely frustrated and gives up.

We've all done this, right? It's important to confirm that the person complaining is actually looking for advice before offering it. It's much more likely they are looking for support, understanding, or validation. Offering suggestions at the wrong time may leave the well-intentioned advice giver feeling annoyed, unappreciated, and helpless while the complainer feels misunderstood and rejected. The cycle doesn't end well and, without proper communication, will just continue to repeat itself, leading to even more frustration and intolerance for future complaints.

Complaining has also been shown to be contagious. Hearing about someone's issues may cause the listener to feel like they need a release, so they discuss the event with someone else and subsequently complain about the complaining. It may also lead to rumination for the listener if they are absorbing all these complaints. If I didn't have my own social outlets and therapy, listening to clients all day might prompt me to need an emotional release. Keeping it all in and avoiding sharing makes it even more likely I'll experience burnout and have trouble listening and empathizing in future sessions.

Complaining also tends to lead to the phenomenon of "one-upping," where someone tries to overshadow your complaint with their own. This is when you're complaining about your back hurting and your friend says, "Oh, you have no idea, my foot hurts so bad! I can barely walk." This pattern unsurprisingly leaves both people feeling misunderstood and unheard. Sometimes it can be helpful to share your own experience to normalize or validate someone, but we have to be very careful about engaging in the complaining Olympics.

Talking about the things that upset us is hard. Sometimes it feels painfully negative and overwhelming. But there's also a lot of healing in those moments when we have the space to listen and empathize. I wonder what would happen if we didn't try to run away from these conversations, but instead tried to get deeper into why they're happening and meet people with compassion and understanding.

Is It Worth Complaining About?

Whenever Sam comes to therapy and vents or complains, it's always about the really big stuff in his life—family, work, his health. It's rarely about traffic or the weather. I always know that when he's complaining about something, it's probably important and has some meaning. We can find meaning in the smaller stuff, too, but some topics are particularly loaded. Once we look deeper into the complaint, we're usually able to create a lot of understanding and dialogue about the emotional problem that is hidden beneath it. This is powerful because it gives complaints a purpose. They're a window into someone's world, revealing what they worry about, hope for, and consider important. I can use what most would view

Complaining can give us an expansive view of our psyche.

as complaints to target the treatment, figure out what the person values, and tap into what they're struggling with. Complaining can give us an expansive view of our psyche and it's absolutely worth paying attention to and exploring.

Of course, there are limits to the effectiveness of complaining. It might be helpful to come to therapy each week and use your complaints as a vehicle for change and understanding, but when complaining becomes constant or circular, it's much less helpful. You may find yourself constantly complaining about little moments in your day where you're annoyed or inconvenienced. It's important to recognize if this complaining is actually helping you or keeping you stuck.

I like to divide complaints into categories: "high-level" and "low-level" complaints. High-level complaints are those big-ticket items that have a large impact. Low-level complaints are typically daily annoyances or frustrations. You get to decide what is high-level and what is low-level for you.

"Low-level complaints" are when you complain about things like:

- The weather

- Traffic

- Your annoying coworker

- Cold food at a restaurant

- Your feet hurting

- Someone cutting in line at the supermarket

Then we have the bigger complaints—the stuff that really matters. You want to pay attention to your high-level complaints. These are the types of admissions that really mean something and are usually a bid for connection.

"High-level complaints" are when you complain about things like:

- Death and loss

- Infertility

- Racism, sexism, homophobia, ableism, sizeism, or classism

- Illness and disability

- Serious relationship issues, breakups, or divorce

- Family struggles or estrangement

- Career trouble or job loss

- The aftermath of a traumatic event

- Parenting challenges

- Experience of pregnancy and postpartum

- Mental health issues

When we discuss these issues, we mean business. We're talking about the things that matter to us and that have a major impact on our life. When you find yourself sharing about these issues or wanting to vent, listen to that need. It's likely that you need an outlet, some connection, or possibly a major change in your life. Some things really are worth complaining about.

How to Tell When You're Stuck in a Complaint Loop

Sometimes we get stuck in a complaint loop and have a lot of trouble getting out. It usually feels like you're just circling with no way out. This typically happens when there is no available solution, we don't feel heard or supported, or we're having trouble accepting our reality. Getting stuck in a complaint cycle doesn't help and it isn't effective.

Here are some signs you are stuck in a complaint loop:

- You keep talking about the same thing over and over and there's no change in your dialogue or complaints.

- You feel stuck.

- Your commentary about the situation is very black-and-white. (E.g., "There is no other job out there for me. I will always be stuck in this soul-crushing place where my boss yells at me every day.")

- People are getting annoyed, do not want to listen, or express that you've been complaining about the same thing.

- The complaining doesn't lead to any relief or connection with others.

- The complaining is becoming more repetitive and may even feel obsessive or like it's playing on a loop.

If you notice any of these things happening when you complain, there are a few tools you can use.

First, try looking for the gray in the situation. Complaint loops usually feel very black-and-white and will include words like *always, never, can't, won't*, etc. When you notice that you're using this language, look for loopholes. Is there any hope or possibility here? Is there any chance that you don't know for sure? Maybe there is some room for flexibility in your thinking or in the present situation.

Using the word *and* can also be an effective way to maneuver your way out of a complaint cycle. Let's say you are complaining that your mom never listens to you. This may feel very true for you and maybe your mom really "never listens." Using the word *and* can help you feel more empowered. So you might say something like "My mom never listens to me and my spouse does" or "My mom never listens to me and I have friends who do." Allowing yourself to validate the very real complaint about your mom and that it hurts when your mom doesn't listen and then adding on a supportive statement makes the situation much more flexible and less bleak. It allows you to make space for the good, the bad, and the in-between.

Sometimes our complaints are very real and true. If you're dealing with the death of a loved one or a new disability, there's not much gray there. It's painful, it's true, and it's real. Maybe you could find some good or flexibility in the situation, but often we're not ready to see that yet. Toxic positivity would tell us that we should only look on the bright side and find what we're grateful for. We're not going to do that because we know it doesn't work. Instead, you're going to practice something called *radical acceptance.*

Radical acceptance is a distress tolerance skill that was developed by Dialectical Behavioral Therapy founder Dr. Marsha Linehan. Radical acceptance acknowledges that pain is an unavoidable part of life and that fighting back against this suffering typically leads to more suffering. I believe that radical acceptance is the antidote to toxic positivity. When we practice this skill, we are not agreeing with, supporting, or saying we like the current reality. Instead, we are accepting that we cannot change the current facts or situation, even if we do not like it or agree with it. This is something I practice with almost all my clients. I do it in my own life, too.

According to Dr. Linehan, there are ten steps involved in practicing radical acceptance that will allow you to move out of a place of suffering and into a place of acceptance.

1. Observe that you are questioning or fighting reality. ("This isn't fair.")

2. Remind yourself that the unpleasant reality is just as it is and cannot be changed. ("This is what happened.")

3. Remind yourself that there are causes for the reality. ("This is how things happened.")

4. Practice accepting with your whole self (mind, body, spirit). Use accepting self-talk, relaxation techniques, mindfulness, and/or imagery.

5. List all of the behaviors you would engage in if you did accept the facts and then practice engaging in those behaviors as if you have already accepted the facts.

6. Imagine believing what you do not want to accept and rehearse in your mind what you would do if you accepted what seems unacceptable.

7. Attend to body sensations as you think about what you need to accept.

8. Allow disappointment, sadness, or grief to arise within you.

9. Acknowledge that life can be worth living even when there is pain.

10. Do pros and cons if you find yourself resisting practicing acceptance.

We all get stuck in a complaint loop from time to time because, well, life isn't fair and reality is often hard to accept. We are going to be challenged by life's ups and downs for eternity. I know it sounds dark, but it's true. When we expect life to be fair or blame a crisis on our inability to think positively or manifest another outcome, it creates a painful separation between our reality and our mental state. The gap between what is and what we expect it to be is almost too painful to endure. If and when you feel like reality is just too hard to accept or acknowledge, try being compassionate toward yourself and use these skills. Look for the gray in the situation, add that *and* to your complaint, and practice radical acceptance. With practice, you'll move out of the loop.

How to Complain Effectively

The right amount of complaining and complaining effectively will help keep you out of that never-ending complaint cycle. Dr. Robin Kowalski, a prominent researcher of complaining behavior, found that those who complain with the hopes of achieving a certain result tend to be happier. Complaining is most effective when the complainer:

- uses facts and logic

- knows their ideal outcome

- understands who has the ability to make it happen

If you are able to identify these three things, your complaining is much more likely to feel useful and effective, while also leading to a better outcome.

Eight Tips for Effective Complaining

1. Figure out the complaint. What is really bothering you?

2. Identify the goal.
   a. Are you trying to make someone aware of an issue?
   b. Do you want to enact change?
   c. Do you want to be heard?
   d. Do you want to be validated?
   e. Do you want advice?

3. Choose the right audience. Who can help you with this? Is there anyone who would understand or relate? Don't

always complain to the same people. Pick people who can actually validate you or help you with your goal.

4. Decide if it's worth it. Think about the issues that are really important to you and focus on complaining in moderation.
   a. What will happen if you do complain about this?
   b. What will happen if you don't complain about this?

5. Validate that you may want to complain because you're looking for connection. Is there anything else you can share to connect other than a complaint?

6. Write it down. This can be especially helpful if you feel like it's hard to manage your complaints. Research shows that writing helps focus and organize experiences and leads to greater understanding of what happened and how to cope.

7. Be as direct about your issue as possible.

8. Remember that there are real inequities in the world. People may call you "negative" or a "complainer" for bringing them up. There are people who have it worse. Keep talking about the issue and focus on your goal.

The goal is not to eliminate complaining from your life, but instead to make it more effective and adaptive. When we complain effectively, we can achieve the closeness, support, and change that we all crave. As you implement these eight tips for complaining, they will become familiar and easier to use. You may even notice that you move through them naturally and without much effort. You will also probably discover that your complaining becomes much more targeted and goal oriented, rather than circular and frustrating.

Reflection

Take a moment to think about the role complaining plays in your life and how you typically process emotions. Answer the following questions honestly and openly.

- Do you find yourself complaining often? What do you usually complain about? Are they high-level or low-level complaints?

- What role does complaining have in your life? Does it make you feel better or worse? More connected or more alone?

- When you complain, is there something deeper going on?

Everything happens for a reason.

Not everything happens for a reason that makes sense. Some situations don't have a silver lining. Whenever you're ready, choose how you want to integrate what happened and what it means to you.

....

Chapter Seven

How to Support Someone

S upporting the people we care about is actually really simple. Unfortunately, we're often so worried about doing it "right," caught up in our own emotions or experiences, or just haven't been taught how, that we get it wrong or don't even try. This chapter will help you understand how to manage your impact and intent, decipher what type of support might be the most helpful for someone, what real support looks like, and how to listen, validate, and show support. You won't always get it right or perfect (you're human), but you will be equipped with the tools that you need to navigate helping the people you care about most and yourself.

Your Intent Matters. Your Impact Matters More.

Sometimes we try to help and we mess up—royally. Our intentions are completely misunderstood or the other person doesn't want to receive our help. This may happen because the way we helped was rude or abrasive, we weren't listening to what the other person really needed, or the other person simply wasn't ready or willing to accept our help even if it was offered in a gracious and kind way. This happened to me in session with Sam when I tried to interrupt his complaining. I was kind and compassionate. I wanted to help, but he didn't appreciate the way I was helping and it wasn't what he needed. This can be incredibly frustrating when we personally view our actions as kind, generous, or helpful. But if your intent didn't line up with your impact, we need to investigate why.

Knowing what to say and when to say it has become really challenging. I know there are so many rules and it seems like they're always changing. If you scroll on social media, you'll find a litany of posts that appear to declare what is the "right" thing to say and what is effectively "wrong." This book might even add to the feeling that you just can't seem to get it right, and that makes sense. I want you to know that there's no perfect thing to say. Everyone is going to have their own preferences and sensitivities, including you. I hate to be hugged or touched when I'm crying, and you might love it. This is why we have to rely less on scripts when it comes to helping others, and more on our compassionate curiosity.

I'm going to go out on a limb and assume that if you purchased this book, you have good intentions. You clearly want to learn how to be more helpful and supportive. The notion that intentions matter less than impact may be difficult for you; I know it was for me. If you've ever been told that you hurt someone despite your intentions, you may have responded quite defensively. Maybe you said something like:

- "I was just trying to help."

- "I didn't mean to hurt you."

- "You're blowing this out of proportion."

- "I'm just trying to be nice. Can't you see that?"

- "I guess you don't want my help, then."

- "You took that the wrong way."

Sound familiar?

If you view yourself as a kind, helpful, understanding person, it can be really challenging to be told otherwise. It might totally rock your sense of self and make you question your identity. As a therapist, I am trained to listen compassionately and help people. I still get it wrong. So, let's all take a moment and take a breath here. Try to admit this to yourself: I am going to get it wrong sometimes. I'm not always going to know the best way to help or support someone and that's OK. I'm going to keep trying, asking questions, and listening. I will try to refrain from getting defensive and instead try to understand.

Once you accept that you are a human being and you're not going to be perfect or set that expectation for yourself, things get a whole lot easier.

When we talk about intention versus impact, it's important to note that these are not equal forces that can be completely separated. Intention doesn't just get thrown out the window; it matters, and research supports this. In a recent study, participants were administered equal electric shocks. Those who thought the shocks were administered intentionally experienced them as much more painful than those who thought the shocks were administered by accident. People are also more highly motivated to assign blame or punish someone when the harmful act is viewed as intentional. Melanie Tannenbaum, a writer for *Scientific American*, astutely points out how this has been woven into our own legal system. Harsher punishments are given for acts that cause more pain or suffering and the intentionality is taken into account. For example, manslaughter is a homicide that is the unintentional killing of another person. These cases are treated as much less severe crimes than murder. Murder is a homicide that is the illegal killing of another person with the knowledge and intention or desire to do evil. These two crimes carry different sentencing minimums and the intent is highly debated in legal proceedings, despite the impact being the same.

Impact and intent are linked within our brains and it's impossible to separate them completely. Studies show that we are more likely to forgive a crime when the reasoning behind it feels just. For example, you're more likely to punish someone who runs a stop sign because they're trying to hide drugs versus a mom running a stop sign to get home to her sick child. The behavior is the same—both ran a stop sign—but how you view the act is entirely different. Research does not argue that intentional harms are more harmful than unintentional ones; in fact, the outcome is always exactly the same. But it does demonstrate how impact and intent cannot be separated and instead must be looked at together to help us engage in meaningful conflict and develop a deeper understanding about what we need and want.

How to Own Your Part

Let's say someone shared that you hurt them. Despite your best intentions, you missed the mark and said something wrong. I know you're a good person and maybe you didn't mean it, but let's forget all that for now. If this is a relationship that you want to improve, you're committed to working through this conflict, and you're interested in getting to some common ground, you're going to triage the needs of the situation in the order of utmost importance in this moment. This person is hurt and we need to attend to that first, then we can move on to the explanations and understanding part.

If this is an abusive relationship or someone that you're not interested in finding common ground with, that's OK. You're allowed to just disengage and walk away. You do not have to follow these steps for every situation—use your own personal judgment.

Let's start the emotional triage process. If you've just hurt someone, despite your best intentions, here's what to try.

- Swallow your pride for a moment. I know this is hard. Maybe you think they're being totally irrational or you absolutely do not see their side. That is OK. You can validate their perspective without agreeing with them.

- Validate their perspective. Again, you don't have to agree. You just have to validate how that could be true for them. Some options that you can make your own:
  - "I hear you and I want to understand more."
  - "It makes sense that you would feel _____."
  - "I appreciate that you shared this with me."

- Try to understand. When the other person is ready (always ask), it can be helpful to try to reach a deeper understanding about what happened in this situation. You'll want to learn:
  - How you impacted them
  - Why this led to that outcome
  - How things can be different next time

- Repair. The type of repair and the extent is going to depend on the level of the hurt and what transpired. You can:
  - Acknowledge their feelings and what happened
  - Apologize and take responsibility for your part
  - Discuss and agree to a plan to repair and prevent this from happening again

- Share your perspective. Once the other person has had a chance to feel heard and understood, they may be open to hearing about your side of the interaction. Your side may include your intentions and why you did what you did. In some situations, it isn't appropriate to share this, and in others it can be extremely helpful. Try to avoid getting defensive or saying any of those statements listed on page 193.

You may have to take breaks between each of these steps or circle back to a step more than once. That's OK. What matters most is that you're open to listening, learning, and finding out how to do better. And remember, these steps only work with someone who is willing to participate in the dynamic. If you're dealing with an abusive individual or someone who has no interest in helping you understand, all of your hard work will not be well received.

How to Share Without Hurting Their Feelings

Another situation where we often have wonderful intentions, but tend to mess up, is when we're sharing our feelings, concerns, or suggestions with someone. Sharing how we feel (especially when it's really personal or sensitive) can be tricky. Sometimes it helps repair a relationship and brings us closer; other times the other person doesn't receive our message well and it results in a divide.

This is another communication hurdle that you won't always get right, but there are some ways to mitigate risk. Here are some tips to help you share how you're feeling without hurting the other person:

- Try to keep the focus on your own experience and feelings. Avoid starting sentences with "You" and swap it out for "I feel."

- Use a calm tone. Avoid yelling.

- Refrain from name-calling or insults.

- Choose your words carefully. Planning what you'd like to say in advance can be helpful.

- Be specific about how you feel and what you believe is leading to that feeling. Telling a story or giving examples can help the other person understand.

- Think about what your goal is for this conversation. What do you want them to know or understand? What would you like to be different?

- Be willing to hear both sides. If the other person is being respectful and is willing to have a conversation, it may help to hear them out.

- Know that you can plan and say everything correctly and they still may not receive it well or understand. Control what you can.

Again, remember that there are situations where you will say everything right and do it all according to the book and it still won't land well. Work on controlling your side of the narrative. We cannot control how someone else receives us, but we can do our best to share in line with our own values. If you shared something and it was hurtful or the other person misunderstood, you can reflect back on this list and see how you did. It's also OK to ask them how you can deliver this message more effectively next time.

The Essential Ingredients

Supporting ourselves and others isn't really about saying the "right" or "perfect" thing. How the words come out will depend on who you're talking to, the topic, and the environment. But you can strive to include these four ingredients in your communication:

- Curiosity

- Understanding

- Validation

- Empathy

Curiosity means we're always learning about the people around us and ourselves. We're learning about what makes us feel safe and supported, how we like to be helped, and what we need in moments of crisis and struggle. Because these are not fixed qualities, what we need and want will always be evolving throughout our lives. Curiosity is asking questions, being open to change, and knowing that we will never be done with getting to know ourselves and others. Curiosity opens the door to understanding, validation, and empathy. You can show curiosity by:

- Asking open-ended questions like "Can you tell me more about _____?" or "I'm listening if you want to tell me about what happened today."

- Using active listening that includes nonverbal cues like nodding, eye contact, and paying close attention to the conversation without distractions.

Understanding is what happens after we've used curiosity. Will we ever fully understand what we need or what other people expect from us? Probably not. But we can continue to seek understanding and knowledge. Understanding isn't the same thing as agreeing. I can understand why you might feel that way and still not experience that feeling myself or agree with it. Understanding is simply using your curiosity to paint a picture and trying to gain insight into the why, the how, and the what. It's making room for the possibility.

- Not assuming that you know how they feel just because you've been through a similar situation.

- Asking questions to make sure you understand how the other person feels, like "It seems like _____ was the hardest part for you, yeah?"

- Continuing to let them share until you both feel like an understanding has been reached and not rushing the process.

When we understand something, we can validate it. Like understanding, validation is not the same thing as an endorsement. It simply means that you can see how something is possible and recognize it in yourself or someone else. This might be challenging at first, but it is absolutely possible. I know it's possible, because I do it every day for a living.

You can sit with someone, validate their experience, and not completely agree with them. When I started my training to become a therapist I learned about something called unconditional positive regard. It means that the therapist has and shows overall acceptance of the client by setting aside their own personal opinions and biases. Validating involves making space to listen and understand how you or someone else feels in their unique experience. It's allowing yourself to understand that your experience and their experience can be true at the same time. I don't always agree with what my clients say. Maybe the choices they make are not the choices I would make in my own life. That is OK. I can still hold space in the room, encourage them to share, and validate their experience. I can see them as unique humans with individual experiences. Validation sounds like:

- "It makes sense why you feel that way."

- "I get why you'd react that way."

- "That is an understandable feeling to have, especially in this situation."

After you've used curiosity, developed an understanding, and validated, then empathy arrives. Empathy is making space for the feelings, understanding them, and allowing the feelings to exist. Everything makes sense in context. When we learn about why a person is the way they are, we're able to develop empathy and understanding.

We can also see things from another perspective and develop an alternative perspective to the situation that is more compassionate and less judgmental. You are demonstrating empathy when you ask questions, try to understand, and validate someone. You can also try:

- Listening and eliminating distractions

- Sharing about a time when you felt the same way and normalizing their reaction

- Refraining from offering suggestions and just allowing them to be with the feelings

- Thanking them for sharing with you

- Continuing to reach out and connect

As you support yourself or someone else, try to focus less on saying the right thing and more on these ingredients. Ask yourself:

- How can I get to know this situation better?

- Is there anything I don't understand about how they're feeling or what they're going through?

- How can I help them feel understood and supported?

- What words or actions might show empathy in this situation?

If you lead with curiosity and seek understanding, the validation and empathy will flow naturally.

How to Be an Effective Support Person

If you're reading this book, you probably enjoy being helpful. Maybe you identify as an empath or a helper. You might also feel a sense of accomplishment or pride when you help others. Sometimes, when we're trying to help, we get so caught up and focused on feeling like we're a "good" helper, rather than being an effective helper. There is a difference between the two.

This is where intent and impact come back into the picture. You need to make sure that your intent is good and your impact is also in line with what is needed by the other person. If we don't know what someone needs or even care to ask, we're often helping because it feels good to us and not because we actually want to remedy a problem.

So, what makes an effective support person? Here are a few key ingredients:

- Good listening skills

- The ability to ask about and identify what the other person needs

- Strong boundaries

How many times has someone cut you off mid-sentence and eagerly asked "Oh my gosh, but have you tried ____?" I know it's happened to me a million times. We're so eager to help or fix that we don't spend time getting to know what the person believes they need or want. If you want to be an effective support person, you have to develop excellent listening skills. This involves asking about and listening for:

- What the person is struggling with

- What resources they have access to

- What they have already tried

- What they are asking for in that moment (Hint: it might not be a solution, but rather a listening ear and some compassion.)

The more you're able to listen to and understand the needs of another person, the more likely you will be able to assist them in a way that is most helpful for them.

Strong boundaries are also essential for helpers. There was a time where I genuinely thought it was my responsibility to fix things for everyone. If something challenging was happening to a family member, I had to carry it, too. I had to make it alright. At the beginning of my career, I had trouble leaving my clients' pain at the office. I had to be equally dragged down by it or it meant I was "insensitive" and "didn't care." Things I read and saw on the news would stick with me for weeks. I felt guilty for enjoying my life when things in the world were "bad." It was hard for me to enjoy life. Everything was black-and-white. Good or bad. I judged people who were able to seemingly forget about what was going on and constantly asked myself, "How do they not care?" It was absolutely unsustainable, and I knew something had to change.

I have learned that you actually don't have to help everyone, and it would be impossible to do so. You may have to set limits with people when you don't have the energy, resources, or qualifications to assist them, and that is OK. In fact, it's the healthy and ethical thing to do. When we are honest with those who need our assistance, they can move on to other people and resources that are more readily available to help them. Some situations might call for help from a professional or someone with more experience in this area. Directing someone to other resources or saying that you can't help doesn't mean that you don't care or that you're abandoning them. It means that you are trying your best to provide them with the right resources, while also giving yourself the ability to set limits and care for yourself.

Here are some ways to tell someone you don't currently have the energy, resources, or ability to help them:

- "I'm so sorry this is happening. I had a rough day and feel like I can't be the best support to you right now. Can I call you tomorrow?"

- "I don't think I'm the best person to help you with this. Have you thought about reaching out to _____?"

- "This topic is really hard for me to talk about."

- "I really want to support you and I'm feeling drained right now. Can I let you know when I have the space to talk about this?"

- Wait to respond until you're ready. Note: If someone is suicidal or thinking of harming themselves and you feel that you cannot help them, it's important to direct them to the right resources. This might include contacting the National Suicide Prevention Lifeline; calling a trusted friend, therapist, or family member to help; or contacting emergency services.

- "Have you ever had one of those days when you're overwhelmed and need time for yourself? That's me today. I'm afraid if I try to give you advice or listen I won't do a great job. Can I check in with you (insert a time)?"

- "I want to be there for you and support you. I don't think I have the bandwidth to do it right now and I know I will later after I get some sleep. Do you feel like we can talk about this (insert a time)?"

- "I really want to support you, but I need to focus on this (project/whatever) right now. Can I check in with you later?"

- "I don't feel comfortable talking about this topic with you. Is there someone else you can share this with?"

Of course, there are certain situations where you may need to help even when you don't have the mental energy, especially if you are a parent or caregiver for someone who relies on you. The ways that you're able to set boundaries will be largely dependent on your relationship with the person, the resources you have access to, and the situation. Try to focus on what limits and boundaries you can set and what areas are within your control. Even with boundaries, you may still experience strong emotions when something happens to someone you love. But boundaries will prevent you from overstepping or suffering more than necessary. They will allow you to focus on helping the other person and effectively listen to their needs.

Remember, the goal is to make space for the pain, not to carry it. When you make space, you sit with the person, empathize, acknowledge, ask where you can be of service, and validate. Taking on their pain will feel heavy and burdensome. It also won't help them or you.

You can ask yourself these questions whenever you're being drawn to help or fix something for someone else:

- Are my boundaries being violated when I try to help?

- Do I feel emotionally or physically drained after helping?

- Is the assistance I'm offering working?

- What is motivating me to help in this way?

- Am I becoming resentful because of my role in this situation?

- Do I feel like I have to prove my worth through helping?

- Am I the right person to offer assistance in this situation?

- Have I asked the other person how they would like to be helped?

- Is the assistance I'm offering causing me to lose other things I value?

- Is helping causing me to feel helpless and/or unappreciated?

Being an effective support person really comes down to listening, seeking understanding, validation, empathy, and strong boundaries with yourself and others. It's OK if you don't always say the right thing; you're not a Hallmark card. You're human. Take the pressure off yourself to always be perfect and say or do the right thing. Lead with those essential ingredients and you'll be amazed at how the smallest gestures and phrases help you and those around you.

To Be Human Is to Be Negative

Supporting other people and listening to complaints can be really challenging. When we're not able to fix something or a topic is overwhelming, we may be tempted to eliminate that person from our lives or simply refer to them as "negative." But humans are inherently negative by nature and it helps keep us alive.

Our tendency to pay more attention to the bad stuff and overlook the good stuff isn't an accident—it's a product of evolution that is necessary for survival. The human brain's main function is to look out for danger and keep us alive, not to make us happy. This is why constant positive thinking can actually be both toxic and dangerous. Without a little negativity, we'd all be really lost.

Way back when, paying attention to the bad, dangerous parts of human existence was literally a matter of life or death. The people who could sense danger and react quickly were much more likely to survive. The world has changed a lot since then, but our brains have stayed very much the same. This is why we may see threat in places where it doesn't really exist or have disproportionate reactions to certain events. Your brain cannot distinguish between what is a real threat and what is a perceived threat. I know, it's confusing. But the more you're able to understand negative thinking and its purpose, the better you'll get at identifying when that primitive way of thinking is kicking in for you and others.

Humans are also prone to something called the negativity bias.

This means that negative impacts have a much greater effect on our brains than positive ones. In a study conducted by psychologist John Cacioppo, people were shown pictures of either positive, negative, or neutral images. Negative images produced a much stronger response in the cerebral cortex than the positive or neutral images, meaning people were much more likely to remember the negative stimuli. There is also greater neural processing in the brain when we're presented with negative, dangerous, or threatening stimuli. Humans tend to:

- Remember traumatic experiences more than positive ones.
- Remember insults more than compliments or praise.
- React more intensely to negative stimuli.
- Think about negative things a lot more than positive ones.
- Respond more to negative events than positive ones.
- Learn more from negative situations or outcomes.
- Make decisions based on negative information more than positive information.
- Dwell on what we may have to give up to achieve a goal instead of what we might gain.
- Focus more on negative information about a new acquaintance.
- Store negative memories in long-term memory more often than positive ones.

With our brains' insistence on focusing on the negative, no wonder it's so hard to be positive all the time! We have to accept that our brains are just trying to keep us alive and safe. Then we can find new ways to operate in the modern world that don't cause us to see failure or threat in places where it doesn't even exist.

No, You Can't Cut All Negativity Out of Your Life

There are thousands of articles online encouraging us to "cut negativity" from our lives, and I find it pretty entertaining. When I hear this, I think, *What does that mean?* Are you not going to talk to anyone who is negative or complains? What topics are off limits? With everything you just learned about the brain, I think we can agree that eliminating all negativity from your life is not only impossible but dangerous.

When people say they want to eliminate negativity, I find that they actually mean they just don't want to struggle or be bothered with anything that makes them feel bad or uncomfortable. This statement is usually used as a reason to not work on yourself, to eliminate people from your life, or to ignore blatantly obvious issues in the world. It's extremely dangerous for our relationships and will result in ending relationships with people who aren't abusive or toxic, but are just going through a hard time.

If you cut everyone from your life who is exhibiting any negativity, you will never form the types of close bonds that develop through struggle and hardship. Now, you absolutely should evaluate relationships, and possibly end them, with people who don't treat you well, are abusive, or don't value your relationship. But that isn't negativity. Negativity may show up as depression, a difficult life event like losing a parent or getting fired, going through a transition, or struggling with a health issue. It's not always toxic or abusive. It's usually just life, and life gets hard sometimes.

When you're thinking about "cutting all negativity out of your life," you might want to ask yourself:

- Am I having trouble articulating my boundaries here?

- Is there something about this topic or person that feels threatening to me?

- Is this issue or person bringing up a feeling for me?

- What do I think will improve in my life if I cut out this negativity?

- Is there anything I can learn from this before removing it from my life?

- Am I setting a boundary or running from an important issue?

- Why do I want to live a life with no negativity?

- If I were dealing with an issue like this, what would it be like to have this person cut me out of their life?

This doesn't mean we have to just accept that we're going to be negative all the time. It means we can work with what we've got and try to create more mental and emotional flexibility. We can also help ourselves feel more safe. Here's how:

- Pay extra attention to good things. We know that noticing the good stuff is much harder than noticing the bad. Make sure you really take it in, focus on how it feels, even write it down. Writing it down can help you integrate the memory and focus on it, and you can look back on it in the future.

- Monitor your self-talk. Self-talk is often what perpetuates a lot of our negative thinking. We say things like "I'll never succeed" or "Everyone hates me." Whenever you have thoughts like this, see if you can pay attention to them and question them.

- Reframe the situation. Some call this putting your thoughts on trial. Pretend that you are a lawyer and investigate your thoughts. Would they stand up in trial beyond a reasonable doubt? Look for the gray. Is there another way to understand what's happening?

But I Just Can't Stand "Negative" People

I know that a lot of negativity can start to wear on you. It's understandable that someone may want to surround themselves with happy, beautiful, positive things. But the world is really messy sometimes, and there's stuff all around us begging for our attention and demanding that we feel something. If we all ignore these calls, the world will never change and our relationships will barely scratch the surface. This doesn't mean that we need to surround ourselves with negativity and respond to every single call for help. You are allowed to set boundaries. And I'd like to reframe how we view "negative people" in our world.

I actually don't really believe in negative people. I believe there are people who:

- feel unsafe

- are struggling

- have been hurt

- haven't learned they're allowed to experience "good" emotions, too

These types of people usually have more negative thoughts and rely on negative thinking to cope. But they're not "negative people" who can never change and need to be eliminated from our lives. Again, being negative and being abusive or hurtful are two completely different things. Not dealing with negative people or cutting them out of your life is not the same thing as setting a boundary with someone who hurt you or continues to hurt you. You are allowed to set boundaries with these people, and it's important that you do so. What I'm referring to is our classification of people as negative when they:

- talk about challenging feelings

- discuss real inequities and issues in our world

- call us out for hurting them in some way

- trigger challenging feelings in us

Negativity has become a catchall word for things we don't like or don't want to face. We call someone "negative" as a way to silence them or absolve ourselves of responsibility. Is negativity annoying sometimes? Oh yeah. But it also forces us to recognize what is important, to repair our relationships, and to create change. Without it, we'd be totally lost. We may want to silence the person talking about a social justice issue that's important to them because it bums us out and makes us not want to address our own privilege. We may want to skip that talk about our friend's health because it makes us face our own mortality. We would rather not hear about our friend's job loss because it leads us to feeling helpless and ineffective. There are so many reasons why negativity and complaining may bother you. Most of them have everything to do with you and nothing to do with the other person. Because, let's face it, we're all a little negative sometimes.

If you're being pulled to label someone as negative, it may be helpful to ask yourself some of these questions. They'll help you decipher if this person is really just being negative or if it's something else that needs more attention.

- Are they triggering a difficult emotion in me?

- Are they a reminder of someone else I know?

- Are they forcing me to look at the issues they're complaining about or discussing?

- Do I not like what they're pointing out in me?

- Do I feel helpless when they are sharing their thoughts?

- Is this person harming me or just bothering me? (There's a difference.)

- Is this behavior considered abuse and do I need to set a boundary with this person?

- Are they struggling with something that is causing their thoughts to be more negative?

Hard feelings are normal, and we all have them. We know that we need these feelings and thoughts to live. If you didn't have anxiety, you would probably be dead. If you didn't experience sadness, you wouldn't know what was important to you. If you didn't complain, nothing would ever get fixed.

Sometimes I wonder: What if negative people just need more empathy and more understanding? What if that is the key to helping them become more optimistic? What if every time we cut someone out of our life for being too negative, we miss out on an opportunity to learn something about ourselves?

Talking about real things is hard. Sometimes it feels really negative. But there's also a lot of healing, progress, and understanding being developed in those moments. I wonder what would happen if we didn't try to run away from these conversations, but instead tried to get deeper into why they're happening. We have to acknowledge issues if we want them to change. When we give people space and validation, they are much more likely to feel better and in turn become more positive. We can't use a positive platitude to make an issue disappear; it will still be there. It will likely get worse. Sometimes we are being hurtful to others and we need to evaluate our behavior. Negativity and complaining give us access to all of this information and open the door for change.

How to Deal with People Who Complain a Lot

Constant, unrelenting positivity and happiness often hinge on the ability to detach and distance yourself from anything that threatens that feeling. If you can avoid every bad thing in the world by turning off your TV, censoring your conversations, staying away from certain people, and just living your life—you are among the very, very lucky few. It's OK to be both grateful for this and aware that it's not always the norm.

We all have a right to turn away from things to recharge and rest—it's necessary. You cannot and should not consume news or distressing content all day every day. As a therapist, sometimes my days are really difficult because of the stories I'm hearing. I have to find space to turn away from it so that I can return to it all the next day. If I continued to think about it all and immerse myself 24/7, I'd burn out and be totally ineffective.

But what about the people who are living it? What about the people who can't just turn it off or look away?

It's not our responsibility to carry that for them, but having more empathy and a deeper understanding of their world can impact how we classify their behavior and change the way we view them. When we imply that others just need to have a better attitude or think happier thoughts, it's worth asking:

- How much of their lives can they not escape or turn away from?

- What am I able to turn away from that might be a daily reality for someone else?

- How can I protect myself and still have empathy for others?

- If I had to face these types of issues daily, would it impact my mindset?

Dealing with hardship and struggle is not necessarily "being negative." There is a big difference between someone discussing their grief and someone who complains about the food at every restaurant. It's important we distinguish between the two.

Remember Sam from chapter six? Sam loved to come to therapy to complain. He was looking for connection and validation, and knew that the therapeutic space would offer him that. When I flipped the script and started offering advice, I totally got in the way of Sam's processing. It wasn't what he needed or wanted at that moment. Complaining can become bothersome when it's repetitive or when we just don't know how to respond to the complaint. Earlier in the book we discussed how complaints can often make us feel helpless and force the listener into fixing mode. If you have someone in your life who seems to complain often, there are many ways that you can respond to complaining while it's happening. Some are better than others. I'll walk you through some of the worst and best ways to respond to a complaint.

Before you respond, it may be helpful to walk yourself through a few of these self-reflection questions.

- Is there a way I can support this person?

- Can I validate them?

- Do I share the same worries and concerns?

- Is there validity to what this person is sharing with me? Am I the person who gets to decide or know what is valid in this situation?

- Would I feel hurt, confused, or another challenging emotion in this situation?

- How would I want someone to respond to me?

- Do they just need time to process or is this an ongoing theme?

- Is this person truly complaining or are they hurting, grieving, etc.?

- Is this a systemic or common issue that many people deal with?

The answers to these questions will help you decide how you

should respond. The options below are the most common ways that people respond to complaints.

Agreement or Disagreement

Depending on the complaint, you may respond with agreement or disagreement. Agreeing isn't always the best way to respond and disagreement doesn't always mean you're being cold or aloof. You don't have to agree with what someone is saying to validate them, either. So, if I'm complaining about the cold temperature in the room and you're hot, you can say "Oh, it makes sense that you're cold. You have a tank top on!" You're not necessarily agreeing, just validating my experience and my truth. You can also totally disagree. A lot of people assume that if they're going to validate a complaint, they have to agree with it. In that same situation, you could say "That's strange, it's eighty degrees in here. Why do you think you're cold? Could you be getting sick?" Whether you're agreeing or disagreeing, you want to make sure that you're validating the other person's reality. This one can be really effective.

Justification or Denial

People may also respond to complaints with justification or denial. These are really typical responses in relational complaints, and they just create further division. Let's say you complain that your partner never does the dishes. They might respond with a justification like "You never ask me to and I'm just so busy!" Or they might just totally deny your complaint with, "That's just not true. I do so much for you." Justification and denial rarely work as a response to a complaint because they put the other person on the defensive. It typically ends up an argument where you're both complaining instead of listening to each other. I would avoid this one as much as you can.

Sympathy and Problem-Solving

Sympathy and problem-solving are really common responses to complaining. I find sympathy or empathy works really well. You can actually end a lot of complaint loops with a quick empathetic response like "That makes sense" or "I get that." Problem-solving gets tricky because if someone doesn't want it, it won't land well. Make sure that the other person actually wants advice or solutions before you offer—trust me.

Countercomplaints

Another way we respond to complaints is with countercomplaints. This is when one person complains and you offer another complaint. I might say "My feet hurt so bad" and you respond with "Oh my gosh. Me, too. I need to get these shoes off." This type of countercomplaining is actually pretty effective when done well. It's best for lower-level complaints where you know that your complaint is on par with the other person's. It's not great when someone is experiencing troubling or distressing emotions because it may result in a one-upping situation or complaint comparison. I would reserve these for smaller issues and avoid comparing major losses, traumas, or other types of distress. It can often make the other person feel like you're drawing comparisons or don't really understand.

Stay Neutral or Ignore

The last way you can respond is by remaining neutral or just ignoring the complaint altogether. Yep, that's right: you don't have to respond to every complaint. Sometimes people complain because they want to experience that catharsis we talked about. They're actually not looking for anything concrete from us. When someone complains, it's OK to just keep the conversation moving. This can again be really useful when someone has low-level complaints like how bad traffic was on their way to the restaurant. I might respond to this by saying, "It's great to see you."

What If I Really Do Need to Cut This Person Out?

There are going to be people in your life who you will need to cut out for a variety of reasons. Maybe their negativity is constantly directed toward you and your life, or they're abusive, want you to fail, or never make space for your feelings no matter how compassionate and understanding you are. There are relationships that are not safe and you aren't able to communicate in the manner I've described in this chapter. Again, you do not have to associate with or empathize with people who constantly hurt or abuse you. Trust yourself to identify those relationships and make that distinction when needed.

You are also always allowed to tell someone you don't have the space or ability to help. Sometimes that is the compassionate and empathetic response. You might be going through your own stuff, don't have the time or resources, or simply aren't the best person to help. It's OK to identify when someone's mood or presence isn't helpful for you right now. Boundaries are your best friend here, and there are many ways to tell someone that you don't have the space to help them at that particular time.

We're All a Little Negative

Let's validate that we all complain. Some of us could complain less and some of us need to work on using our complaint muscle more. But complaining is not something that's going away or that we need to permanently abolish. It has a real purpose in our lives. It connects us, tells us what's important, and helps us process our feelings. Sometimes, we just need to complain and that's OK.

It's important to remember that:

- It's normal for things to upset you. The world can be an overwhelming and scary place sometimes.

- Talking about the things that are important to you is not "negativity."

- Some people won't be able to support you when you need a listening ear. That doesn't mean that you're being too much or should stop sharing. Find your people.

Reflection

- What am I looking for in a support person? What makes me feel most supported?

- What types of support and help am I best at offering?

- What types of support or help tend to deplete me the most?

- Am I usually the one who gives more or less in my relationships? What might be contributing to this dynamic?

Life will never give you more than you can handle.

Life may give some of us more than we can handle on our own, and that's OK. Bad things don't happen to people because they're "strong enough." You will figure it out and you can acknowledge that life is not fair. Some challenges are too large for one person. Ask for help and remember you don't have to be strong all the time.

Chapter Eight

Discrimination with a Smile

Toxic positivity and the pursuit of happiness have been a driving force in Western culture for centuries. Throughout this book, you've learned how these forces infiltrated society and continue to play a strong role in religion, healthcare, science, and the workplace. This phenomenon isn't new and it has continued to uphold the very systems that hold many of us back.

I want to warn you, this chapter may be difficult to read or confusing. The research was challenging for me to comprehend at first. I knew toxic positivity ran deep, but I didn't really understand how powerful and pervasive it was. It can be hard to comprehend how something this "happy" can help maintain many of these challenging issues. I hope this chapter will illustrate the multitude of ways that toxic positivity continues to uphold oppressive systems within our world.

This chapter may also be a difficult journey for anyone who is disabled, dealing with a chronic illness, a person of color, living in a larger body, transgender or queer, a woman, or embodies another type of marginalized identity. Take your time reading this and feel free to skip over anything that feels too heavy or doesn't apply.

I'll be touching on some really personal topics in this chapter, and I want to share my own identities to help you better understand my perspective. I'm an American, white, heterosexual woman in my early thirties. I am of Hispanic heritage and my mom is a first-generation Cuban American. I am married and my husband is Jewish; so is my child. I always had food on the table growing up and never had to deal with real financial insecurity or lack. My individual experience with racism, homophobia, antisemitism, sizeism, ableism, and classism is basically nonexistent because of how I present, and I'm extremely aware of that privilege. As a woman, I have, of course, experienced sexism in its many varieties and I am a wife, daughter, and friend to people who have experienced many of these forms of prejudice.

I know that my own experiences will impact how I discuss these issues. Because of this, I have relied upon and integrated the perspectives of many insightful researchers who specialize in some of these areas of study or embody one or more of these identities. I have had the privilege of working with a wide array of people as a clinician in a diverse city like Miami, and I've also used that experience to inform this chapter. I'm not an antiracism educator. I'll never know what it's like to navigate the world in some of these bodies or identities. But I am intimately familiar with the ways that toxic positivity keeps us stuck and suffering. My experience and research has taught me that all too often:

- Instead of making healthcare more accessible, we're encouraged to use our mindset to cure disease.

- Instead of improved accessibility for the disabled, we're celebrating and encouraging "inspiration porn."

- Instead of creating more gender equality, we're focused on spreading the ideal of the "happy housewife" and the woman who "has it all," while demonizing the "angry feminist."

- Instead of focusing on racial equality, we're pushing the narrative of "Let's all just love each other" and continue to ask "Why can't we just all get along?" without making any real change or efforts.

- Instead of making room for different body types and eliminating diet culture, we say we're promoting body positivity and body love while refusing to change any of the systems that maintain these ideals.

- Instead of embracing the many identities and relationships that humans participate in, we've given people living on the margins just enough to "be happy," and we get upset when they're not grateful.

- Instead of creating more financial equity in our world, we push get-rich-quick books, idealize overworking, encourage "financial manifestation," and imply that hard work will always lead to success.

Let's dive in and look at how toxic positivity maintains these systems and how we got here.

The Ultimate Gaslighting

At its core, toxic positivity is a form of gaslighting. It tells people that what they're feeling isn't real, they're making it up, and that they're the only one who feels this way. We see this gaslighting play out in many positive thinking texts.

Luis was a big fan of the Law of Attraction when I met him. It's ironic that he chose me as a therapist, given my public denouncing of this "law" all over my social media. Our first sessions revolved around manifestation and controlling thoughts. As a human, I was cringing inside, but decided to tread carefully and listen to how these tools were benefiting him and what role they played in his life. Honestly, it doesn't really matter if I approve of how a client copes. If it's working for them and not harming anyone else, then it's an effective skill and I am going to collaborate with them on achieving their goals. I don't have to like it.

What I found most interesting was that Luis kept coming back to therapy week after week, despite his immersion in the Law of Attraction, his dedication to the beliefs, and his undying confidence that it would work. He kept choosing to sit with a therapist who clearly wasn't a big fan of these beliefs. I figured there was something else going on here, and I decided to wait until he was ready to talk about it.

After a few weeks, Luis started sharing about his trauma from childhood. He never mentioned any of this during his initial consultation; I was under the impression he wanted to improve his motivation and become more productive. Luis presented as a calm, cool, and collected male in his thirties who simply wanted to sleep better and "live his best life." But I could tell we were chipping away at that facade and with a little more effort and a deliberately slow pace, we would get somewhere.

Luis and I started talking about his relationship with his grandmother who raised him. His mother died when he was ten and he never met his father. In our first session, Luis reported that his mom had passed away and he didn't know his father, but overall he had a "fine, normal childhood." Can you see the pattern of denial here?

Over the course of several sessions, Luis started to share stories of abuse, neglect, and food insecurity. His childhood resulted in an insatiable drive to never feel the way he felt as a kid ever again. He would always have money in the bank, food on the table, and a home filled with positivity and peace—no matter what. This is how Luis and the Law of Attraction first became acquainted. He was searching for control and a foolproof way to make sure that he never experienced those emotions again. The tenets presented him with that promise on a silver platter.

"The most powerful law in the universe" would give him money, positive thoughts, and happiness in droves if he could just focus on the good in his life and forget about everything else. Luis used his typical unrelenting work ethic and did everything "right." He read the books, thought the thoughts, and distanced himself from everything that could possibly detract from the promise of abundance—including his own past. There was just one problem: he couldn't run from it all. The childhood trauma he experienced was still with him, and the avoidance only intensified its grip on his adult life. He would soon find himself sleeping less, isolating, and having trouble with intense flashbacks and memories. Luis would also begin to blame himself for everything that ever happened to him and felt like an immense failure. He was in deep, and had no idea how to get out.

The toxic positivity that we see in so many manifestation and Law of Attraction texts isn't new. It's a classic form of gaslighting that tells people that there are no victims, only cocreators. Toxic positivity insists that prejudice is invented, your thoughts can literally make you sick, and that everyone gets exactly what is meant for them. I know Luis isn't the first or last client who will sit on my couch and wrestle with these ideas. We're all looking for a way to achieve happiness and control over our lives, and these ideas are enticing and captivating—until they're not.

Health and Happiness

Health and happiness have long been associated with one another. Disability or illness is often seen as a burden, and it's rare that we see disabled or chronically ill bodies represented as regular people in the media. The images we're fed usually trend toward "inspiration porn" or stories about the one who, despite everything, found a way to beat the odds, achieve it all, and find happiness within the able-bodied definition of happiness. We demand positivity from the disabled and ill or assume that they're bringing the pain on themselves and want to be a victim.

Members of this group have long been a target of happiness politics. Eugenic researchers promised individual and collective happiness through their methods and believed that emotional states other than positivity were bad for evolution. They ignored the current social, political, and economic challenges in favor of a simplistic view of illness and happiness. If you didn't agree with the philosophy or methods, you were deemed "unscientific" and ultimately ignored or cast aside. The eugenics movement appeared in the United States in the early 1900s, and it was an extremely dark time for people with physical and mental illness or disabilities, who were ultimately blamed for the unhappiness of the entire society.

Throughout the height of the eugenics movement, people who suffered from serious illnesses were denied medical treatment to "test their resilience." It was commonplace to use "scientific studies" as evidence that helping the disabled would ultimately be harmful for the entire population and lead to more illnesses and unwanted social conditions. People with disabilities were deemed "feeble-minded." They were believed to have improper emotional states, a lack of emotional control, and "high temper, uncontrollable fits of anger, feebleness of will, inability to hold a social idea permanently in mind, lack of ambition to provide good homes as their neighbors . . . and mental drive." The central thesis was that these individuals would detract from the happiness of the larger population. So, the proposed solution was to get rid of them and pretend they never existed—all in the name of the pursuit of happiness.

Some psychologists at the time believed that the elimination of "feeble-mindedness" would result in an enormous improvement in happiness and achievement in every community. Feeble-mindedness was just another name for anyone mentally or physically ill who couldn't become the current definition of a contributing, productive, happy member of the current society. This meant locking away, sterilizing, or killing anyone who threatened the happiness of the larger society. The mentally and physically ill were seen as one of the largest threats to happiness during this period, and many believed something had to be done.

The relationship between health and happiness continues to be extremely problematic today. Books that promote the Law of Attraction or manifestation often propose that thinking or worrying about illness will actually lead to more illness. They also tend to pose the question, "Have you noticed that those who speak most of illness have more and more illness?" And to answer this question, no, I really haven't noticed this. I've spent my professional career working with people who live with chronic illness and disability, and many of my family members deal with these issues. I have yet to find a correlation between talking about illness and the occurrence of illness. I can't find any reliable data to back up this claim, either.

Illness and disability often result because of a complicated interplay between a wide variety of factors. Here are some of the most common factors that influence our overall health:

- Socioeconomic status

- Distribution of medical care

- Environmental toxins

- Social support and meaningful relationships

- Job strain or unemployment

- Discrimination

- Religious beliefs

- Gender

- Social influences

- Tobacco use

- Food access and quality

- Alcohol and drug consumption

- Sexual safety and safe-sex education

- Disease screening practices

- Stress and available coping skills

- Early childhood development and exposure to stressful events in childhood

- Immune system function

- Neurotransmitters, neuromodulators, and hormones

- Genetic predisposition

Many of these contributing factors are ignored or simply left out of the conversation. It's much easier to pretend that we have full control over our health, and this is how toxic positivity continues to support detrimental beliefs about health, disability, and illness. Instead of looking at why people get sick and stay sick or trying to make a world that disabled and chronically ill people can better navigate, we focus on thoughts and positivity as the main avenue for healing disease. We have little tolerance for the "negativity" that is experienced when acknowledging and recognizing the disabled body as human, multifaceted, and worthy of respect.

In Sara Ahmed's *The Promise of Happiness*, she eloquently

describes how certain bodies become objects that either threaten or challenge our happiness. Things become happy or unhappy depending on the meaning that we give them. Throughout history, the frail, disabled, or ill body has been labeled as unhappy. The presence of a body that does not fit the traditional narrative of health forces us to confront our own mortality and health. It makes us recognize that health isn't guaranteed to anyone and we don't have full control over our health outcomes. When that imperfect body experiences and displays emotions other than positivity or happiness, we may want to distance ourselves even further.

Take a moment to think about how we respond to people living with illness or disability. We often expect them to acclimate and join the able-bodied world or get out of the way. People who are ill are told to "Get well soon" and we tend to celebrate the disabled only when they've found a way to overcome all obstacles, inspiring happiness and positivity through their accomplishments and resilience. People often only tolerate disability and illness when it is associated with their version of what it means to be healthy and happy. It becomes almost impossible to separate health from happiness, so if you're not going to be healthy, you better at least be happy. It's cruel and completely unachievable for so many.

Health and happiness are not a package deal.

Removing toxic positivity from conversations about health, illness, and disability requires us to confront a lot of difficult realities. We all may become temporarily or permanently sick or disabled at some point in our lives. Health and happiness are not a package deal, and someone can live a full and meaningful life without meeting all the predetermined characteristics of "health."

What if we simply allowed the disabled body to exist as it is? With all of its emotions, flaws, and multitude of facets. What if we allowed people to express themselves and share their feelings, regardless of their health status? Maybe real health and wellness means focusing less on helping people feel happy in spite of their struggles and more on how our world can accommodate and embrace people of all abilities and diagnoses. I know this is a tall order, but what if our collective well-being depends on it?

The Un-Gratefuls

The pursuit of happiness is also intimately tied to racism and anti-immigrant sentiments. Perceptions of "the angry Black woman," "melancholy migrants," and "the model minority" have persisted throughout time. Once again, science was used to impose this agenda in the name of the pursuit of happiness.

In the early 1900s, emotional self-control was seen as the greatest virtue and scientists proposed that certain races had better emotional regulation than others. The more a group could control their emotional reactions, the more civilized they were. Scientists and leaders sought to create "evolutionary utopias marked by happy controlled societies filled with happy efficient people." This meant eliminating any groups that expressed too much negativity and impeded the pursuit of happiness.

The image of the "melancholy migrant" became very popular around this time. If you appeared depressed, it was viewed as a sign of lack of intelligence. Pre– and post–World War II immigrants in the United States, especially Jewish immigrants, were actually encouraged to keep quiet about their traumas and war-related distress. If they weren't positive, they would be deemed unfit and lacking emotional regulation, ultimately threatening their place in society. Immigration assessment also emphasized positive adjustment and productivity, while ignoring the circumstances and influences, like trauma, that often led immigrants to struggle with their emotional regulation or rapid assimilation into a new culture. Immigrants were held to an extremely high standard and risked expulsion from the larger group if they did not perform or did anything to threaten the overall happiness.

Toxic positivity was also used regularly to silence and cast off Indigenous and Black citizens. Scientific studies were produced that argued Black people had smaller brains and that this is why they were prone to more emotional dysregulation and were ultimately a threat to happiness. The goal was to prevent "racially fit individuals from developing racially poisonous emotional states and behaviors, which could harm the hereditary stock of future happy and healthy societies." This meant separating racial groups in an attempt to "protect" white people from the poisonous nature of other groups.

We continue to see happiness and positivity used as weapons

within communities of color and among immigrants. Responses like "Can't we all just love each other?" and "We're all just one human race" are typically used to silence and discontinue conversations about racism in favor of more "happiness" and cohesion. The problem is, we're only prioritizing one group's happiness and comfort while ignoring and silencing the other. We're effectively saying, "Sorry you're hurt, but your negativity and response to racism is really bumming me out, so could you stop?"

Within positivity culture, immigrants and people of color are expected to be grateful for what they have and to embrace the pursuit of happiness developed by the Founding Fathers. If they aren't satisfied, they can just "go back to where they came from." Conversely, we use positive stereotypes to reinforce the types of people who have "made it" within this system. We say things like "She's a strong Black woman" without questioning why Black women have to be so strong and why we expect this from them. The happy, contributing immigrant is celebrated for achieving the narrow definition of the American dream against all odds. Even though these stereotypes are positive and often given as compliments, they become quite restrictive for anyone within the group who can't live up to them.

Today, racism and other forms of oppression have been reduced to a set of individual choices. If someone can't make it within this world, it's because they're not trying hard enough. They're too negative, too angry, too abrasive. They're not professional enough, complain too much, aren't grateful, and they can't get along with others.

Pointing out flaws in the system is often viewed as dissidence. We reward an unrelenting positive attitude and the ability to not ruffle any feathers or disrupt the norm. Positivity is how we maintain the systems and "keep the peace," but the foundation is starting to crack and some people aren't willing to tolerate it anymore.

Getting angry and expressing dissatisfaction is often one of the most effective ways to create change within a society. Positive platitudes and the pursuit of happiness are ultimately being used as tools to keep people submissive and quiet. There is a prevailing belief that if you make too much noise, you're threatening my happiness and I have a right to pursue my happiness. Anything that threatens that pursuit is negative, inconvenient, and must be discouraged.

The Happy Housewife and the Angry Feminist

Women have long been trapped within the confines of toxic positivity.

The role of the "happy housewife" epitomizes the early modern definition of what it means to be a woman and the intense expectation to always remain positive, even under extreme circumstances. Ultimately, the happy housewife is a fantasy. She is the beaming, well-kept woman washing dishes and smiling as she puts dinner on the table every night. She is both fulfilled and inspired by her domestic duties and seeks to improve the overall happiness of the entire family. When this image was popularized throughout the

1950s and 1960s, many women were actually already in the workforce. It was only women, primarily white women, who had the time and money to stay home who could access this fantasy. Betty Friedan was a critic of the happy housewife fantasy and proposed that women should be liberated from the home. But according to feminist author bell hooks, she did not address who would ultimately take over the woman's duties when she left the home to find happiness. Ultimately, it would be women of color who entered the home to relieve the white woman of her burden. This meant that only some women were liberated from the weight of the happy housewife fantasy and others were relegated to continued attempts and failures at pursuing it.

The problem continued when white women were promised happiness outside of the home, yet couldn't find it there. Their work was still not seen as equal with men in both pay and responsibility. Sexual harassment was prevalent and women were still saddled with the majority of household management. Happiness continued to be used as a tool to maintain the traditional gender roles in society. Happy families had clean and beautiful homes, heterosexual marriages, well-behaved children, and a patriarchal figure who was gainfully employed in a respectable career. It was assumed that if you had these things and followed the path, you would be happy—and if you weren't, there was something wrong with you.

Anyone who chose to opt out of this system was seen as negative and a "killjoy." Sara Ahmed discusses the image of feminist killjoys in her work *The Promise of Happiness*. According to Ahmed, the feminist is deemed negative when they disrupt the happiness fantasy that is promised through typical gender roles and the ideal family. She's often described as unlovable or unable to "fit in" with the other women. The truth is, the feminist is just paying attention—and when you pay attention you notice that there's a lot to be dissatisfied with.

Today, we see the image of the happy housewife playing out in a lot of different ways. On social media you've probably become familiar with "mommy bloggers." There are thousands of accounts dedicated to creating and perfecting the image of the perfect mother and housewife. The image centers around a happy marriage, well-dressed and -behaved children, and an Insta-worthy home. A positive attitude allows them to flourish. The content is curated extensively and the line is blurred between fantasy and reality. We think we can achieve it because we don't see the story behind the image. The curated content allows us to feel just close enough to the person that we don't question anything.

There is also the new image of the woman who "has it all." She's successful in her career, a wonderful mother, and a devoted wife. It's important that this woman continue to maintain the gendered expectations for the home, child-rearing, and marriage or she will inevitably be criticized. The focus is on making it all look effortless and doable. Again, the lines between fantasy and reality are extremely blurred here, and it's possible to believe that with the right attitude and a lot of hard work, you can do it, too.

I've fallen into the trap of both of these ideals. Toxic positivity among women is rampant, and complaining about motherhood, marriage, or career is often met with a lack of sympathy and deemed negative or ungrateful. I've learned that there's not one happy place that we all get to if we do everything "right." Maintaining all of this is so hard, it's almost impossible, and we certainly can't do everything all the time. It's OK to ask for help. It's OK to complain and be grateful. It's OK to challenge everything you've been taught about being a woman and create a totally new definition for yourself. Despite what you've been told, happiness does not lie within strict gender roles or norms.

Look Like Me and You'll Be Happy, Too

I can't remember a single day of my life where I didn't have a negative thought about my body. It's such a common occurrence that it took me many years to even notice when I was engaging in body checking or criticizing myself physically. Honestly, I thought it was just part of being a woman. My mom did it; all my friends did it. It was how we bonded and a major topic of conversation.

Diet culture and body acceptance landed on my doorstep through social media. I slowly opted out of only following size 0 influencers drinking green juice in exchange for more diverse and anti-diet voices. Recognizing diet culture all around me has been jarring, eye-opening, liberating, and terrifying all at once. It has also illuminated how often we associate thinness with health and happiness. Health cannot be separated from the pursuit of thinness or toxic positivity. They are inevitably linked and help support one another.

The diet culture industry is a billion-dollar mammoth that sells the promise of happiness, health, and thinness. Ultimately, they profit off our insecurities while also promising to liberate us from them. We are continuously told that if we just beat one more insecurity or lose one more pound, we will finally be happy. Many of the ads used to sell these products are overwhelmingly positive. Smiling, upbeat people bound across beaches and laugh among friends. You're sold a fantasy that is never going to be realized because happiness doesn't exist within another body. If you've ever looked back at a picture of yourself and thought, "Wow, I looked great there!" and then remembered how much you beat yourself up during that time of your life, you know exactly what I mean. It's a never-ending cycle. Sonya Renee Taylor, the author of *The Body Is Not an Apology*, asked an important question at one of her live talks to help us deal with this type of predatory marketing of happiness and thinness. She asked the audience to consider, "Who is profiting off of my insecurity?" I love this question and have used it often in my own battle with diet culture and when working with therapy clients. When we ask this question, we can step away from the promise of happiness, health, and thinness and really look at how our insecurities are being weaponized to sell a product that promises us something it will never deliver.

Toxic positivity has helped maintain diet culture, but it also shows up in the realm of body positivity. When I first encountered the idea of "body positivity," I was intrigued. I thought it was much better than constant criticism of our bodies and certainly better than diet culture, but it just went too far. All of a sudden we were expected to love our bodies, compliment them, and speak kindly to them and about them. After a lifetime of diet culture, body positivity just seemed way too far out of reach for me and my clients. This is how toxic positivity can show up in such a complicated way. Similar to positive affirmations, trying to feel too positive about our bodies too quickly can lead to a lot more harm than good. This is why I've transitioned away from body positivity and embraced body neutrality and acceptance.

The term *body neutrality* started gaining traction online in 2015. It became widely known when Anne Poirier began using it at her retreats in 2016. Body neutrality is about seeing your body as it is and acknowledging how it helps you move through the world. All bodies have value despite their capabilities or limitations. Instead of focusing solely on loving your body, you are encouraged to let go of strong emotional reactions or judgments toward it. This has been shown to help with anxiety, depression, and overall well-being. Having this mindset means you will still have negative thoughts about your body and slip back into old patterns, but you're also able to understand that this happens in a world that prioritizes thinness in the name of health and happiness and isn't a sign that there's anything wrong with you.

They're Happy with So Little

We treat happiness as a measurable objective despite many of us having opposing definitions of what it truly means to be happy. Ultimately, the people with the most power and resources are the ones who get to decide what happiness is, how it's achieved, and who is allowed to achieve it. This has resulted in a belief that the happiest nations are the richest and most industrialized, despite this reality being starkly contradicted in many assessments.

We also argue that wealth equals happiness and the more one is able to achieve, the more likely they are to be happy. There are so many things that we are told will lead us to happiness—a new car, a new house, a new pair of shoes. All of these keys to happiness cost money, and the belief that they'll relieve us from existential pain is deeply ingrained in our psyche. Advertisements prey on the desire for a fulfilling, happy life and promote products that will supposedly satisfy that need. But what happens when they don't? We go looking for more. Maybe we just didn't get the right car, or we need a bigger house, or the shoes went out of style. No matter what the object, the happiness is fleeting or it never arrives at all.

The relationship between wealth and happiness is complicated, and many researchers have attempted to explain why some people are happy with so little and others are miserable with so much. In a recent research study, higher income was associated with less daily sadness but not more daily happiness. Money doesn't necessarily make someone happier, but it can lead to more control over one's life and ultimately less sadness.

It's clear that toxic positivity plays a role in maintaining current class structures, equating wealth with happiness, and putting immense individual pressure on the poor to overcome their challenges in the pursuit of happiness. We often hear "Look, they're so happy with so little" as a way to explain happiness among groups of people that do not have access to some of the opportunities or resources in the Western world. There's an immense pressure to achieve wealth and happiness through conventional means or accept that you can't and be happy anyway. Forced gratitude shows up often here, and people who have been given the bare minimum are expected to be constantly positive and grateful that they have any access at all.

If someone is unable to achieve wealth and happiness, their attitude is usually the first thing we blame. They weren't trying hard enough, they didn't think positively, they need to manifest wealth, they are living in a "victim" mindset. We rarely look at the systems that keep people stuck and instead choose individualistic reasons that are rooted in toxic positivity. The way to combat toxic positivity within conversations about wealth is to remove money from the equation entirely. We know that access to certain resources like a safe place to live, quality relationships, proper food and nutrition, and healthcare are the building blocks of well-being. Without these things, people will continue to struggle with both happiness and achievement. If we turn the conversation away from wealth and happiness and instead focus on how we can make things more equitable on a basic level, people will be able to achieve their own form of happiness.

As Long as You're Happy

We also see toxic positivity show up in the LGBTQIA+ community. Initially, these identities were viewed as sinful and were hidden away from mainstream society. Leaders and researchers used the same approach that they used with immigrants, the disabled, and communities of color with this population—remove them from society so they don't threaten our happiness.

As conversations about queerness moved into the mainstream via literature, books about gay people only had unhappy endings. A queer person could live out their identity, but there was no way this was going to result in happiness. In an attempt to make things easier, we encourage people to be who they are while also aligning themselves as closely as possible with our predetermined paths to happiness. Sara Ahmed accurately calls these paths toward happiness "happiness scripts." These are the manuals for how to be happy. They tell us what to do and how to live. If you follow them correctly, you will be happy.

In an attempt to make things less difficult for LGBTQIA+ individuals, we encourage them to "be who they are," but to also align themselves as closely as possible with heteronormative happiness scripts. This means you can be whatever you want, but if you really want to be happy you still need to get married, have children, and get a job. We may have embraced more identities and types of relationships, but the pressure to be happy and positive about those choices has never been greater. People say, "I don't care who you love. I just want you to be happy." There's an insistence that this "choice" to live differently better lead to happiness, and if it doesn't, well, then something is wrong. We have these grand expectations even though heterosexual couples are getting divorced and reporting that they're unhappy in their marriage at alarming rates. If you are transgender or queer and end up in an unhappy relationship, the reasoning is usually that you must've just gotten it wrong. Maybe you aren't this person after all? Maybe this unhappiness means you were just confused. There's an immense pressure to find happiness at the end of these decisions.

This pressure also extends to identity in general. There is an expectation that when someone in the LGBTQIA+ community announces or embraces their identity and shares it with the world, it will be the answer to all of their problems. Suddenly they will be happy, filled with pride, and all their mental health struggles will disappear. And for some, maybe this is the key and it helps alleviate distress, but for so many it's only one piece of the puzzle. If you continue to struggle, again your decision is doubted or questioned. Maybe you got it wrong. Maybe you are heterosexual; maybe you're not trans. Are you sure this is what you wanted? Positivity, happiness, and an unwavering commitment to your decision are the only acceptable outcomes.

If we want to remove toxic positivity from our conversations about LGBTQIA+ identity, we have to view people as human be-ings with a multitude of emotions that go beyond their identity, their relationship status, or how they refer to themselves. Expecting unrelenting positivity and happiness from someone simply because they've been able to express themselves isn't helpful. Instead of equating identity or self-expression with happiness and positivity, we can look at it as one small, ever-evolving piece of how someone feels and who they are.

Whatever you decide to do in life, make sure it makes you happy.

Live a life that challenges you, fulfills you, has meaning, and brings you moments of joy. Open yourself to all emotions and experiences. Discover what you value and follow it until the end, knowing that sometimes life is going to hurt and that's what makes it worth living.

Chapter Nine

How to Find Fulfillment in a Difficult World

Yes, life is tough and we still don't have to struggle all the time. There is space for happiness and pain. We can make room for it all without dismissing the good, the bad, or the neutral.

Throughout this book you've learned how incorporating the right amount of complaining and gratitude, negativity and positivity, and empathy and boundaries can lead you toward a more fulfilling life. We know that slapping on a smile and a positive attitude isn't going to fix the big issues that pop up in life. We have to find a way to make space for the good and the bad while living a life that is in line with our unique values, goals, and talents.

Opt Out of the Quest for Happiness

The first thing we can do is opt out of the constant quest for happiness. I know, it sounds counterintuitive. How will I ever be happy if I'm not pursuing happiness?

Let's start with a few questions:

- If happiness is the key to a meaningful life, why are so many of us still miserable?

- Has the constant pursuit of happiness actually brought you more happiness?

- What have been the happiest moments of your life? Were there any other emotions present during these moments?

- Are you waiting for an aha moment when you finally feel happy?

Our culture has been obsessed with promoting happiness for centuries and it doesn't seem to be working. Research demonstrates that the more people see happiness as a goal, the less happy they are. Americans invest more time, energy, and money into finding happiness when compared to any other country, yet we aren't getting any happier. According to the General Social Survey, there has been almost no change in American happiness levels since 1972.

So, despite our best efforts to become happier and all the focus on happiness, something isn't working.

When you google "What is the secret to happiness?," 480 million results instantly appear. Each promises a different path toward this elusive goal. While there is some overlap on these lists—relationships and gratitude are usually mentioned—every list reports being rooted in science, yet offers a different perspective or methodology. Each of the studies also looks at different populations and there is little attention paid to cultural factors that may impact what actually influences and leads to happiness among different groups.

What you need to be happy is constantly evolving and changing depending on where you live, your gender, your age, and other factors. We've been sold the idea that the path to happiness isn't individual or fluid. It's a standardized list of culturally approved practices that, when done correctly, will lead you to the promised land. The most common path is to be healthy, go to school, graduate and get a job, get married, have children, retire, and die. While you're checking off those boxes, it's expected that you will show gratitude, have the right mindset, and not complain. Unfortunately, so many of us are either unable to achieve these milestones or simply do not want to.

I'm someone who has followed this path to a T. I've done everything as expected, on the "right" timeline, and it's led me to a lot of fulfillment and moments of happiness because it's what I wanted and valued. If that's your path, too, great. But as a therapist, friend, and family member, I've seen this path, and the constant need to find happiness, destroy people and leave them feeling like failures when they can't achieve it through the prescribed means.

So, what if happiness isn't always achievable for everyone through the paths we've been given? What if we've been sold something that is unidentifiable, unmeasurable, and ultimately unachievable? This is why I'm encouraging you to opt out of the quest for happiness altogether. Instead, focus on finding fulfillment, forging your own path, and living a life in line with your values. Maybe your path will be the "traditional" one and maybe it won't be. Both are OK. Both are worthy.

Living a Value-Driven Life

Finding fulfillment requires living a value-driven life. A value-driven life is quite different from a happiness-driven life. In a happiness-driven life, we're focused on maintaining a good mood, seeking out only positive and happy experiences, and achieving happiness as the ultimate goal. A value-driven life allows you to prioritize what is important to you and find a path to get there. It makes room for the fact that living in accordance with our values doesn't always mean feeling happy or good, but it is in alignment with who we are and what we want.

A Happiness-Driven Life

- Only concerning yourself with things, ideas, experiences, and people that will enhance your happiness.
- Following the right path that will lead to happiness, even if it's not what you want.
- All painful or negative thoughts are threats to your happiness and need to be eliminated.
- Anyone who complains, doesn't agree, or struggles is taking from your happiness.
- Happiness is promised to anyone who fully dedicates themselves to achieving it. If you haven't, you're not trying hard enough.

A Value-Driven Life

- Knowing the things, ideas, experiences, and people that we value in our life.
- Knowing your values will motivate you and help illuminate your path.
- Your pain, complaints, and distressing feelings often point directly to your values and can be accepted.
- You can choose relationships based on your values and recognize that relationships aren't easy or good all the time.
- Living in accordance with my values will lead me to moments of happiness and struggle. It can all exist at the same time.

Acceptance and Commitment Therapy is one of my favorite tools for achieving a value-driven life. ACT helps people develop psychological flexibility, which is the ability to exist in the moment and recognize feelings and bodily sensations, even if they are uncomfortable or painful. This type of flexibility pushes us to view our emotional experiences without judgment instead of making decisions about life based on avoiding whatever discomfort or pain we are experiencing. Constantly seeking out happiness or positivity can lead to so much avoidance, especially when we feel like our negative thoughts are going to lead to our demise. So instead of just looking for what brings about the "good" feelings, we are going to focus on what gets us closer to our values.

The first step in living a value-driven life is discovering what your values are. Remember, these values may change throughout your life and what you commit to today can always change. Values are not meant to serve as rules or directives. They are guideposts that help you make decisions and feel more fulfilled.

Start by thinking about your values in each of these four domains of life—work/education, relationships, personal growth and health, and leisure. Not everyone has the same values and there is no "right" answer. In each of these columns, ask yourself:

- What's important?

- What do I care about?

- What would I like to work toward?

- What values were instilled in me by my culture and my family? Are those values important to me as an individual today?

Your value will not be a specific goal. Instead, it is the way you would like to live your life. For example, maybe your goal is to spend at least one night a week with your spouse. Being an attentive and interested spouse would be the underlying value and you would embody that value by spending time with your spouse.

If you have trouble coming up with values, think about some of the goals and behaviors that you'd like to achieve and what value might be prompting that. There are also several great value lists online that will help you start thinking about your personal values.

If you notice that you are someone who says they value family time but you're spending eighty hours a week at work, you may need to get creative with how you're going to embody that value. This exercise can also help you question your values and identify if closeness with family is actually more important than work or if you just think it should be. It's a good idea to consistently check in with your values and how you're living. Your values are going to change as you age and as your life shifts. It's OK to make adjustments as you go. When you're living in line with your values, things will be much more fulfilling and they will make sense. It won't always feel "good," but you'll know that you are in alignment with who you want to be.

Validation and a Kick in the Butt

One of the worst things about toxic positivity is that, when used in the wrong moments, it denies what we're feeling and makes us feel worse. But sometimes we do need a little boost to get through. Maybe you're just one step away from completing a big task or you got a little lost on the way to your next goal. It happens, and compassion and validation go a long way in these moments. We also might need to give ourselves a little pep talk from time to time.

If you take away one thing from this book, I hope it's this lesson: There is immense power in knowing when you need compassion and when you need a kick in the butt. Sometimes you need one and sometimes you need both. We have to know how to dance the delicate dance of validation and pushing ourselves. Too much of either isn't going to end well.

Having compassion for yourself and validating your feelings is really important. I can't say that enough. It's probably why validation is trending right now. So much so that if we (or someone else) challenge an emotion, try to show a different perspective, or maybe don't view it as 100 percent true, it's seen as gaslighting. And I get it, validation is very important. It's super helpful. And sometimes, we lean in too hard, get lost in the feeling, and have trouble finding our way out. We have to make sure that we don't go from toxic positivity to over-validation and get stuck.

Let's start with what validation is and what makes it helpful.

Validation may seem like an endorsement, but it's not. When you validate, you're really just saying:

- I honor the fact that I'm a human who is going to feel a lot of things.

- Maybe it doesn't make sense right now and it's something I'm experiencing.

- I'm going to feel this, let it pass, and then either investigate it or move on.

Validation is usually what we need during a difficult moment. When talking my clients through something challenging, I like to use validation before I move into the pep talk. It gets us through the storm and then when we come out on the other side, we can decide what we want to do. Maybe:

- It was a bad day or moment and you're going to move on.

- The reaction was rooted in something else and you want to investigate it.

- You just needed some more support before looking at it differently or moving forward.

Validation is the start of the process. It leads us toward understanding or moving on. It works a lot better than shame, guilt, or toxic positivity. And when we're willing to use validation AND take on a new perspective or learn something, a lot of good can happen.

The key to living a fulfilling and value-driven life often lies in knowing what to validate, for how long, and when to give yourself a little push. Try starting with validation until there isn't any shame or guilt and you've accepted that what you're feeling is what you're feeling. Then, if there's something you really want to achieve or get done, maybe you can try to push yourself a little. Move slowly here and notice if any of those guilt-shame feelings pop up. If they get worse or you don't feel motivated, it might be time for a little more of a push. Here's what that might look like:

- "I'm feeling (name) and I'm allowed to have this feeling. This project must be really important to me, so I'm going to stay focused."

- Noticing the feeling and choosing to take a walk or engage in some other quick reset, then getting back to what you need to do.

- "I am having a feeling and I will allow myself to process this later. Right now, I have to get through this."

- Thinking of reasons why you need or want to complete this task.

There's no exact formula here (wish I could give you one, trust me).

This is all about getting in touch with your values and your goals and learning how you respond to validation and a little bit of a push. Everyone needs a different ratio of each, depending on the situation.

Take a Break from the Self-Help Spiral

When you start striving to live a value-driven life instead of a happiness-driven life, you may be tempted to go full throttle and figure this out today. It's what so many of us do in an attempt to be better and feel better. I want you to do the opposite of what almost every self-help book out there has probably told you. I want you to go slow, take breaks, and even quit from time to time.

I know, it seems counterintuitive, but work with me here.

I think there's immense value in introspection and working on ourselves. So much so that I wrote an entire book and post every single day on social media about how we can improve our mental health. All of us have things that we could work on or learn about ourselves to make us better partners, family members, friends, and coworkers. Sometimes we have to do this work if we want to maintain certain parts of our life. Mental illness and mental health issues are real, and they require work, treatment, and often professional help to heal.

But I've also seen a dangerous pattern on Instagram and within the walls of my office—people are becoming obsessed with healing. It's their main focus. It's part of everything they do. It's like orthorexia (an obsession with healthy eating), but for the mind. There's a fixation on finding the "root cause" of everything, self-diagnosis, and figuring out what trauma or event from childhood led to this behavior in their adult life. There's always a book, list, quote, or course that promises to help you achieve your best self. What seems like a positive quest for self-improvement goes awry when people are left feeling flawed, failed, or less than.

Here are a few key signs that a healing or self-improvement practice is negatively impacting someone:

- Constantly finding new things to improve or fix

- Thinking there is something wrong with you

- A belief that you have to "heal" or change to be accepted

- Feeling bad when you're not constantly pursuing wellness, health, or improvement

- Judging people who aren't constantly choosing to heal or improve

- Not allowing yourself to feel or experience challenging emotions because it would mean you're not "healed"

- All or most of your daily activities revolve around health or improving yourself in some way

These are just some of the signs that I have noticed when someone becomes so deeply invested in healing that they aren't fully living. They're working toward this place that doesn't really exist. I could check off a lot of the features on this list during certain parts of my life. In my training to become a therapist, I was so focused on showing up as my "best" self for clients. I wanted to be the most healed, integrated version of myself because I was supposed to be the leader and role model in the room. I also wanted whatever I was feeling to go away so desperately that I became hyper-focused on fixing, healing, and learning. Now I'm able to float in and out of therapy. Read a self-help book when I feel like it and put it down when I don't. I can actually enjoy life, experience my emotions, and be aware when there's stuff I need to work on. Now, it's a process of acceptance and growth, rather than a race to perfection.

There's always something to fix or improve. You actually don't have to pursue health, happiness, or wellness all the time. You're allowed to:

- Watch TV or movies with no educational component

- Do nothing

- Sleep

- Eat food just because it tastes good

- Read something for fun

- Move your body for enjoyment

- Scroll mindlessly on social media

Seriously, eat the cookie. Watch the movie. Read the book. Not everything you do has to be about improving your health, your knowledge, your job, or your body. It's OK to just be. There's no finish line or trophy for being the most improved. In fact, you'll probably find that every time you "fix" one thing, the world starts begging you to work on another. Your "best" and "happiest" self will always be out of reach. It's not a destination you can reach and enjoy. In fact, you are your "best self" when you're messing up and trying your best, setting boundaries and considering others, apologizing when needed, asking for help, and living life on your terms. A complete lack of awareness and zero work on the self is dangerous. It can cause you to lose relationships, jobs, and other facets of your life. But an obsession with self-improvement isn't the answer, either. Don't be afraid to rest and enjoy exactly where you're at—even if that means putting down this book and unfollowing me on Instagram. Seriously, do it if you need to.

It's OK to just be.

Sometimes a Little Positive Fantasy Does Help

There are some situations where a daydream or a positive fantasy can be immensely helpful. Gabriele Oettingen, a researcher and author of *Rethinking Positive Thinking*, conducted several studies on the impact of positive fantasies and dreams on motivation. Her research consistently led to one clear outcome: "Positive fantasies, wishes, and dreams detached from an assessment of past experience didn't translate into motivation to act toward a more energized, engaged life. It translated into the opposite." This means that if you have no prior evidence that you can achieve this goal and rely on dreams or fantasies to achieve it, you will not feel more motivated. If I imagine that I am going to become a professional basketball player at five feet four and thirty years old, imagining it, dreaming about it, and faking it 'til I make it likely aren't going to get me there.

While her research did clearly indicate that dreams and positive fantasies typically did not improve motivation or lead to better outcomes or performance, these fantasies did serve an important purpose in other situations. Dr. Oettingen found that dreams or positive fantasies help distract us while we're waiting or getting through something quite difficult. This strategy has been used by combat soldiers, prisoners, and those at the end of life. It is the most useful when there is no opportunity for action and we just need to get through. It provides short-term pleasure and keeps people engaged in the process of waiting.

Positive fantasies and daydreams can also be used to mentally experience a goal or explore possible avenues. Let's say you are daydreaming about becoming a lawyer. Maybe you imagine yourself sitting at a big desk, hanging out with your coworkers, and making a big salary. But then your mind drifts to the late nights and time spent in front of complicated documents. You start questioning whether this fantasy is really enjoyable or not. Maybe you don't actually want to be a lawyer? Positive visualization exercises can take you on a journey of figuring out what you actually want and what you don't want. From there, you can take action.

Positive visualization and fantasies can help us:

- Deal with pain in the moment

- Be patient

- Persevere in situations where we have no control

- Experience short-term pleasure

- Clarify our dreams and desires

The key is to know when to use positive fantasies and when we need to act.

Finding What Works for You

Just like there's not one path toward a fulfilling life, there is not one thing that works for all people. As a therapist, I know this to be absolutely true (and there are very few things I'll say that about). We are all walking around the world with different values, identities, life experiences, and cultural norms. You will never find a psychological theory or self-help practice that is going to apply to everyone in the world—and that is OK.

Opting out of toxic positivity and the constant pursuit of happiness requires us to look at how we want to live and how those choices impact the people around us. It means prioritizing our own needs and recognizing that everyone around us has their own values and ways of living. We don't get to determine what happiness is for anyone and we can still hold people accountable, set boundaries, and protect our own energy. Opting out of the happiness rat race ultimately creates space for all of us to forge our own paths and quit arguing over what should be making us happy. It's liberating.

When we opt out of the predetermined path toward happiness, we gain access to so much more. You'll get to feel all of it—joy and pain, comfort and discomfort, growth and stagnation. You'll be able to ride the waves of life and know that there isn't this final happiness destination. This is it. This is what we've got—and all the feelings, ups and downs, changes, and chaos certainly make the ride much more interesting.

Final Note: Reminders About Being Human

I 've shared a lot with you in this book. It's likely that some of your beliefs about happiness and positive thinking were challenged within these chapters. I appreciate you reading and being open. I know that isn't easy.

I wanted to leave you with a few notes about being human as you embark upon the world with all this knowledge and some tips for identifying toxic positivity out in the wild. I hope this helps you integrate what you've learned.

- You are going to feel a wide variety of emotions. Some will feel better than others. Embrace them all.

- The single biggest predictor of human happiness is the quality of a person's relationships. Give back to the people you love, set boundaries, and remember that relationships are never perfect.

- You are going to complain and feel negative. This doesn't mean that you are vibrating at a "low frequency" or have "bad vibes."

- Life will challenge you and it will reward you.

- Happiness isn't always the optimal emotion for every moment.

- You didn't manifest everything bad in your life, and you play an integral role in healing from it.

- Not everything is possible for every person, and your life will have meaning, purpose, and joy.

- The universe might give you more than you know how to handle right now and someway, somehow, you will find the people, places, and things that you need to manage it all.

How to Spot Toxic Positivity in the Wild

Toxic positivity is all around us, and it's important that we don't view everything happy or positive as toxic. Remember, positivity isn't toxic, it *becomes* toxic. I created this chart to help you navigate toxic positivity versus helpful positivity in the real world.

Toxic Positivity

- Tells people they shouldn't be feeling what they're feeling
- Implies that people are negative if they can't find the silver lining in everything
- Encourages people to be happy all the time and always see the "good"
- Ends the conversation or relationship because we don't want any "negativity" or "bad vibes"
- Uses phrases or statements that diminish what the person is experiencing in an attempt to help them "feel better" or "get over it"
- Only looks out for the "good" and ignores anything "bad"
- Shames people for having bad days or negative moments

Helpful Positivity

- Recognizes the value of seeing the good and allows people to arrive at their own beneficial conclusions and to take their time getting there
- Recognizes that humans have a variety of emotions, some more challenging than others, and allows people to see the "good" and "bad" sides of a situation
- Has an understanding that not all situations have a silver lining and we will still experience joy
- Encourages emotional expression from others (with boundaries) and from within ourselves, knowing that for some to experience happiness, they often have to process and move through the pain
- Looks out for and recognizes the highs and lows of a situation

So, if you see a sign in a restaurant that says *Good Vibes*, that's probably OK. You're there to have a good time! Toxic positivity would be telling your friend who is depressed, "You really need to work on your bad vibes, they're bringing me down." See the difference?

Not all positivity, happiness, or good vibes are bad. Remember to look out for the timing, audience, and topic that you're discussing. This is the best way to identify if something is toxic positivity.

Acknowledgments

I wrote this book pregnant during a global pandemic. It was the most rewarding and challenging professional experience I've had thus far and I am confident none of it would have been possible without the support and guidance of so many people in my life.

To my husband, your unrelenting support and interest in my work has fueled me throughout this entire process. It is an absolute gift to have a partner who wants you to succeed and is invested in making that happen no matter what. I hope we continue supporting each other personally and professionally for the rest of our lives. We make a great team. Your contract negotiation skills and legal advice were also a great perk throughout this process.

I want to thank my son, who provided me with a constant supply of hormones and emotions throughout this book writing process. You allowed me to tap into feelings I didn't even know were there. Thank you for the insomnia—I got a lot of writing done during those quiet morning hours. I don't know what you'll become, but I will always be proud of you and I hope this book makes you proud of me, too.

To my parents, thank you for showing me that growth and change are always possible. Mom, you are my biggest cheerleader, my best friend, and my constant support. You have supported my Instagram from day one and served as my sounding board for post ideas, biggest defender from internet bullies, and number one spell-checker. Thank you for becoming the parent I always needed. Watching you navigate life has taught me that it's never too late to put yourself first or learn something new. I will never stop calling and texting you ten times a day. Dad, you taught me to create the career I always wanted. Thank you for teaching me to never take no for an answer and to always ask for what you deserve. I know I got my complete inability to follow the traditional path or work for someone else from you.

I have to thank the person who has taught me more about resilience and standing up to toxic positivity than anyone else: my sister. Watching you navigate life, change directions, and become this version of yourself has been incredible. I am so proud of you. Thank you for teaching me something new every day.

To my in-laws, thank you for becoming my new family, always asking questions about my work, and being so excited for me. Most of all, thank you for raising a man who I can always count on. I love you all. And to the rest of my big, Southern Cuban family, I have never felt alone knowing you are behind me. There is no one else like you.

To my editor, Marian; my agent, Laura Lee; and the entire team at TarcherPerigee, thank you so much for believing in this idea and supporting me throughout the entire process. You made it fun and simple. I appreciate your leadership, expertise, and dedication. I will forever be grateful that we were able to work together—I loved every minute.

My Instagram community, you made this book possible with your engagement and support. Thank you for all the likes, shares, comments, and messages. I also have to thank my clients, who inspire me and teach me every single day. It is a gift being able to learn from you all. This book is for you.

And to all my friends, thank you for the endless support. You've shared my posts, asked so many questions about the book, and promised to buy all the copies. Thank you for keeping me motivated on days when I was unsure about where this whole "Instagram therapist" thing was going to go. I am so grateful to have every single one of you in my life.

Ahmed, Sara. "Killing Joy: Feminism and the History of Happiness." *Signs: Journal of Women in Culture and Society* 35, no. 3 (2010): 571–94. https://doi.org/10.1086/648513.

Ahmed, Sara. *The Promise of Happiness.* Durham, NC: Duke University Press, 2010. https://doi.org/10.1515/9780822392781.

Andrade, Gabriel. "The Ethics of Positive Thinking in Healthcare." *Journal of Medical Ethics and History of Medicine,* December 21, 2019. https://doi.org/10.18502/jmehm.v12i18.2148.

Brackett, Marc A. *Permission to Feel: Unlocking the Power of Emotions to Help Our Kids, Ourselves, and Our Society Thrive.* New York: Celadon Books, 2019.

Ehrenreich, Barbara. *Bright-Sided: How the Relentless Promotion of Positive Thinking Has Undermined America.* Waterville, ME: Thorndike Press, 2010.

Recommended Reading

Oettingen, Gabriele. *Rethinking Positive Thinking: Inside the New Science of Motivation.* New York: Current, 2015.

Taylor, Sonya Renee. *The Body Is Not an Apology: The Power of Radical Self-Love.* Oakland, CA: Berrett-Koehler Publishers, Inc., 2021.

Yakushko, Oksana. *Scientific Pollyannaism: From Inquisition to Positive Psychology.* Switzerland: Palgrave Macmillan, 2019.

Chapter 1: What Is Toxic Positivity?

24 **It leads to emotional suppression:** Ruan, Yan, Harry T. Reis, Wojciech Zareba, and Richard D. Lane. "Does Suppressing Negative Emotion Impair Subsequent Emotions? Two Experience Sampling Studies." *Motivation and Emotion* 44, no. 3 (2019): 427–35. https://doi.org/10.1007/s11031-019-09774-w.

29 **"New World":** Ehrenreich, Barbara. "The Dark Roots of American Optimism." Essay. In *Bright-Sided: How the Relentless Promotion of Positive Thinking Has Undermined America*. Waterville, ME: Thorndike Press, 2010.

29 **Arrived in the New World were Calvinists:** Ehrenreich, Barbara. "The Dark Roots of American Optimism." Essay. In *Bright-Sided: How the Relentless Promotion of Positive Thinking Has Undermined America*. Waterville, ME: Thorndike Press, 2010.

29 **Was considered a sin:** Nicole, Riger R. "From the Archives: The Five Points of Calvinism." *Reformed Faith & Practice*, May 25, 2016. https://journal.rts.edu/article/from-the-archives-the-five-points-of-calvinism/.

Notes

29 **In the New Thought movement:** "New Thought." Encyclopedia Britannica. Encyclopedia Britannica, Inc. Accessed June 2, 2021. https://www.britannica.com/event/New-Thought.

30 **Phineas Parkhurst Quimby:** Ehrenreich, Barbara. "The Dark Roots of American Optimism." Essay. In *Bright-Sided: How the Relentless Promotion of Positive Thinking Has Undermined America*. Waterville, ME: Thorndike Press, 2010.

30 **Mary Baker Eddy:** Gottschalk, Stephen. "Mary Baker Eddy." Encyclopedia Britannica. Encyclopedia Britannica, Inc., July 20, 1998. https://www.britannica.com/biography/Mary-Baker-Eddy.

30 **William James:** Duclow, Donald. "William James, Mind-Cure, and the Religion of Healthy-Mindedness." *Journal of Religion and Health*, March 2022. https://doi.org/10.1023/A:1015106105669.

31 **Used to treat physical ailments:** Duclow, Donald. "William James, Mind-Cure, and the Religion of Healthy-Mindedness." *Journal of Religion and Health*, March 2022. https://doi.org/10.1023/A:1015106105669.

32 **Napoleon Hill quickly became:** Hill, Napoleon. *Think and Grow Rich*. Sound Wisdom, 2016.

32 **In 1952, Norman Vincent Peale:** Peale, Norman Vincent. *The Power of Positive Thinking*. Samaira Book Publishers, 2019.

32 **Eugenics was also extremely popular:** Yakushko, Oksana. *Scientific Pollyannaism: From Inquisition to Positive Psychology*. Springer, 2019.

33 **John B. Watson and G. Stanley Hall:** Yakushko, Oksana. *Scientific Pollyannaism: From Inquisition to Positive Psychology*. Springer, 2019.

34 **You can use the power of positive thinking:** Hicks, Esther, and Jerry Hicks. *The Law of Attraction: The Basics of the Teachings of Abraham*. 1st ed. Hay House, Inc., 2006.

39 **"Happier Babies Have an Edge":** Coffey II, John K. "Happier Babies Have an Edge." *Scientific American*, October 16, 2019. https://blogs.scientificamerican.com/observations/happier-babies-have-an-edge/.

40 **The Australian Temperament Project:** Vassallo, S., and A. Sanson (Eds.) "The Australian Temperament Project." Australian Institute of Family Studies, May 30, 2013. https://aifs.gov.au/publications/australian-temperament-project.

44 **Manifestation is defined:** Hurst, Katherine. "Manifestation Guide: How To Manifest Anything You Want In 24hrs." TheLawOfAttraction.com. Greater Minds. Accessed June 2, 2021. https://www.thelawofattraction.com/manifest-something-want-24hrs-less

45 **WOOP tool:** Oettingen, Gabriele. *Rethinking Positive Thinking: Inside the New Science of Motivation*. Current, 2015.

Chapter 2: Why Positivity Doesn't Always Work

51 **Mindset and subconscious beliefs:** Eker, T. Harv. *Secrets of the Millionaire Mind: Mastering the Inner Game of Wealth*. Harper Business, 2005.

52 **Giant dice:** Fairs, Marcus. "Google Has Had Negative Effect on Office Design Says Jeremy Myerson." *Dezeen*, March 10, 2021. https://www.dezeen.com/2016/03/22/google-office-design-negative-effect-interiors-jeremy-myerson/.

53 **Striving for here is groupthink:** Janice, Irving. Essay. In *A First Look at Communication Theory*, 235–46. New York: McGraw-Hill Education, 1991.

53 **Toxic positivity stunts creativity:** Duncan, Cath. "A User's Guide to Creative Tension." Productive Flourishing, June 7, 2010. https://www.productiveflourishing.com/a-users-guide-to-creative-tension/.

53–54 **Visualize possible solutions:** Jiménez, Jacinta M. "Toxic Positivity: The Unexpected Killer of Creativity in the Workplace." LinkedIn, November 27, 2019. https://www.linkedin.com/pulse/toxic-positivity-unexpected-killer-creativity-jiménez-psyd-bcc/.

54 **Empathy for the customer:** Jiménez, Jacinta M. "Toxic Positivity: The Unexpected Killer of Creativity in the Workplace." LinkedIn, November 27, 2019. https://www.linkedin.com/pulse/toxic-positivity-unexpected-killer-creativity-jiménez-psyd-bcc/.

54 **Federal labor laws:** Dahl, Melissa. "Huh, Would You Believe That Forcing Employees to Act Happy Is a Terrible Idea?" *The Cut*, November 7, 2016. https://www.thecut.com/2016/11/forcing-employees-to-act-happy-is-a-terrible-idea.html

56 **A Gallup poll:** Tritch, Teresa. "Engagement Drives Results at New Century." Gallup Management Journal, September 11, 2003. https://www.nova.edu/ie/ice/forms/engagement_drives_results.pdf.

56 **A few simple ways:** Bright, David S., Kim S. Cameron, and Arran Caza. "The Amplifying and Buffering Effects of Virtuousness in Downsized Organizations." *Journal of Business Ethics* 64, no. 3 (March 2006): 249–69. https://doi.org/10.1007/s10551-005-5904-4.

56 **Brain imaging:** Bright, David S., Kim S. Cameron, and Arran Caza. "The Amplifying and Buffering Effects of Virtuousness in Downsized Organizations." *Journal of Business Ethics* 64, no. 3 (March 2006): 249–69. https://doi.org/10.1007/s10551-005-5904-4.

57 **Performance outcomes:** Bright, David S., Kim S. Cameron, and Arran Caza. "The Amplifying and Buffering Effects of Virtuousness in Downsized Organizations." *Journal of Business Ethics* 64, no. 3 (March 2006): 249–69. https://doi.org/10.1007/s10551-005-5904-4.

57 **Committed to the company:** Bright, David S., Kim S. Cameron, and Arran Caza. "The Amplifying and Buffering Effects of Virtuousness in Downsized Organizations." *Journal of Business Ethics* 64, no. 3 (March 2006): 249–69. https://doi.org/10.1007/s10551-005-5904-4.

60 **Diminished immunological response:** Andrade, Gabriel. "The Ethics of Positive Thinking in Healthcare." *Journal of Medical Ethics and History of Medicine*, December 21, 2019. https://doi.org/10.18502/jmehm.v12i18.2148.

61 **Possibly even death:** Andrade, Gabriel. "The Ethics of Positive Thinking in Healthcare." *Journal of Medical Ethics and History of Medicine*, December 21, 2019. https://doi.org/10.18502/jmehm.v12i18.2148.

63 **Ongoing chronic diseases:** "The Growing Crisis of Chronic Disease in the United States." Partnership to Fight Chronic Disease. Accessed June 2, 2021. http://www.fightchronicdisease.org/sites/default/files/docs/GrowingCrisisofChronicDiseaseintheUSfactsheet_81009.pdf.

64 **Live with a disability:** "Disability Impacts All of Us Infographic." Centers for Disease Control and Prevention, September 16, 2020. https://www.cdc.gov/ncbddd/disabilityandhealth/infographic-disability-impacts-all.html.

64 **Research shows that optimism:** Andrade, Gabriel. "The Ethics of Positive Thinking in Healthcare." *Journal of Medical Ethics and History of Medicine*, December 21, 2019. https://doi.org/10.18502/jmehm.v12i18.2148.

64 **Direction in causality:** Andrade, Gabriel. "The Ethics of Positive Thinking in Healthcare." *Journal of Medical Ethics and History of Medicine*, December 21, 2019. https://doi.org/10.18502/jmehm.v12i18.2148.

65 **Well-being is a metric:** "Well-Being Concepts." Centers for Disease Control and Prevention, October 31, 2018. https://www.cdc.gov/hrqol/wellbeing.htm.

66 **Good Vibes Only God believes:** Chamberlain, Dale. "Why Christians Should Beware the Trap of Toxic Positivity." Her & Hymn, November 10, 2020. https://herandhymn.com/2020/06/25/toxic-positivity/.

68 **Play by the rules:** Murray, Kelly M., Joseph W. Ciarrocchi, and Nichole A. Murray-Swank. "Spirituality, Religiosity, Shame and Guilt as Predictors of Sexual Attitudes and Experiences." *Journal of Psychology and Theology* 35, no. 3 (2007): 222–34. https://doi.org/10.1177/009164710703500305.

69 **Their teachings:** Ley, David J. "Overcoming Religious Sexual Shame." *Psychology Today*, August 23, 2017. https://www.psychologytoday.com/us/blog/women-who-stray/201708/overcoming-religious-sexual-shame.

69 **"God is positive":** Ehrenreich, Barbara. "God Wants You to Be Rich." Essay. In *Bright-Sided: How the Relentless Promotion of Positive Thinking Has Undermined America*. Waterville, ME: Thorndike Press, 2010.

69 **Up 9 percent in the same time period:** "In U.S., Decline of Christianity Continues at Rapid Pace." Pew Research Center's Religion & Public Life Project, June 9, 2020. https://www.pewforum.org/2019/10/17/in-u-s-decline-of-christianity-continues-at-rapid-pace/.

70 **Avoid painful emotions and experiences:** Raab, Diana. "What Is Spiritual Bypassing?" *Psychology Today*, January 23, 2019. https://www.psychologytoday.com/us/blog/the-empowerment-diary/201901/what-is-spiritual-bypassing.

70 **In relation to psychological distress:** Levin, Jeff. "Religion and Mental Health: Theory and Research." *International Journal of Applied Psychoanalytic Studies*, 2010. https://doi.org/10.1002/aps.240.

71 **Cheerful disposition and emotional self-control:** Yakushko, Oksana. *Scientific Pollyannaism: From Inquisition to Positive Psychology*. Springer, 2019.

72 **Best and happiest life:** Yakushko, Oksana. *Scientific Pollyannaism: From Inquisition to Positive Psychology*. Springer, 2019.

Chapter 4: Stop Shaming Yourself

115 **Positive thinking is actually counterproductive:** Cooper, Belle B. "Your Positive Work Culture Might Be Making Your Team Less Productive." *Fast Company*, April 25, 2017. https://www.fastcompany.com/40411368 /your-positive-work-culture-might-be-making-your-team-less-productive.

115 **Risk or a difficult situation:** Andrade, Gabriel. "The Ethics of Positive Thinking in Healthcare." *Journal of Medical Ethics and History of Medicine*, December 21, 2019. https://doi.org/10.18502/jmehm.v12i18.2148.

119 **Your already existing values:** Rose, Steve. "Do Positive Affirmations Work? A Look at the Science." Steve Rose, PhD Counselor, July 25, 2020. https://steverosephd.com/do-positive-affirmations-work/.

120 **Potential to be true:** Rose, Steve. "Do Positive Affirmations Work? A Look at the Science." Steve Rose, PhD, July 25, 2020. https://steverosephd.com /do-positive-affirmations-work/.

126 **Control over our emotional experience:** Brackett, Marc A. *Permission to Feel: Unlocking the Power of Emotions to Help Our Kids, Ourselves, and Our Society Thrive.* New York: Celadon Books, 2019.

127 **More distress you'll experience:** Kalanthroff, Eyal, Noga Cohen, and Avishai Henik. "Stop Feeling: Inhibition of Emotional Interference Following Stop-Signal Trials." *Frontiers in Human Neuroscience* 7 (March 14, 2013). https://doi.org/10.3389/fnhum.2013.00078.

130 **The world around us:** Valikhani, Ahmad, Fatemeh Ahmadnia, Alma Karimi, and Paul J. Mills. "The Relationship between Dispositional Gratitude and Quality of Life: The Mediating Role of Perceived Stress and Mental Health." *Personality and Individual Differences* 141 (2019): 40–46. https://doi.org/10.1016/j.paid.2018.12.014.

130 **Conceptualize those events:** Ma, Lawerence K., and Eamonn Ferguson. "Supplemental Material for Does Gratitude Enhance Prosociality?: A Meta-Analytic Review." *Psychological Bulletin*, 2017. https://doi.org /10.1037/bul0000103.supp.

131 **Show or experience gratitude:** Jans-Beken, Lilian, Johan Lataster, Denise Peels, Lilian Lechner, and Nele Jacobs. "Gratitude, Psychopathology and

Subjective Well-Being: Results from a 7.5-Month Prospective General Population Study." *Journal of Happiness Studies* 19, no. 6 (May 30, 2017): 1673–89. https://doi.org/10.1007/s10902-017-9893-7.

132 **Directly predict physical health outcomes:** Jans-Beken, Lilian, Nele Jacobs, Mayke Janssens, Sanne Peeters, Jennifer Reijnders, Lilian Lechner, and Johan Lataster. "Gratitude and Health: An Updated Review." *Journal of Positive Psychology* 15, no. 6 (2019): 743–82. https://doi.org/10.1080/17439760.2019.1651888.

132 **Improve emotional well-being:** Jans-Beken, Lilian, Nele Jacobs, Mayke Janssens, Sanne Peeters, Jennifer Reijnders, Lilian Lechner, and Johan Lataster. "Gratitude and Health: An Updated Review." *Journal of Positive Psychology* 15, no. 6 (2019): 743–82. https://doi.org/10.1080/17439760.2019.1651888.

133 **Struggling with psychopathology:** Jans-Beken, Lilian, Nele Jacobs, Mayke Janssens, Sanne Peeters, Jennifer Reijnders, Lilian Lechner, and Johan Lataster. "Gratitude and Health: An Updated Review." *Journal of Positive Psychology* 15, no. 6 (2019): 743–82. https://doi.org/10.1080/17439760.2019.1651888.

137 **Feeling of gratitude:** Jans-Beken, Lilian, Nele Jacobs, Mayke Janssens, Sanne Peeters, Jennifer Reijnders, Lilian Lechner, and Johan Lataster. "Gratitude and Health: An Updated Review." *Journal of Positive Psychology* 15, no. 6 (2019): 743–82. https://doi.org/10.1080/17439760.2019.1651888.

137 **Compliment others:** Valikhani, Ahmad, Fatemeh Ahmadnia, Alma Karimi, and Paul J. Mills. "The Relationship between Dispositional Gratitude and Quality of Life: The Mediating Role of Perceived Stress and Mental Health." *Personality and Individual Differences* 141 (2019): 40–46. https://doi.org/10.1016/j.paid.2018.12.014.

137 **Moments of intense struggle:** Valikhani, Ahmad, Fatemeh Ahmadnia, Alma Karimi, and Paul J. Mills. "The Relationship between Dispositional Gratitude and Quality of Life: The Mediating Role of Perceived Stress and Mental Health." *Personality and Individual Differences* 141 (2019): 40–46. https://doi.org/10.1016/j.paid.2018.12.014.

Chapter 5: How to Process an Emotion

143 **Significance of the event:** "APA Dictionary of Psychology." American Psychological Association. Accessed June 8, 2021. https://dictionary.apa.org/emotion.

143 **Awareness of the emotion itself:** Lenzen, Manuela. "Feeling Our Emotions." *Scientific American*, April 2005. https://www.scientificamerican.com/article/feeling-our-emotions/.

143 **Consciously or subconsciously:** Cherry, Kendra. "How Does the James-Lange Theory Account for Emotions?" *Verywell Mind*, November 19, 2020. https://www.verywellmind.com/what-is-the-james-lange-theory-of-emotion-2795305.

144 **"Guide one's thinking and actions":** Brackett, Marc A. *Permission to Feel: Unlocking the Power of Emotions to Help Our Kids, Ourselves, and Our Society Thrive.* New York: Celadon Books, 2019.

145 **Our prior experiences:** Barrett, Lisa Feldman. *How Emotions Are Made.* Macmillan, 2017.

145 **Changes what's happening in the body:** Smith, Ryan, William D. Killgore, and Richard D. Lane. "The Structure of Emotional Experience and Its Relation to Trait Emotional Awareness: A Theoretical Review." *Emotion* 18, no. 5 (2018): 670–92. https://doi.org/10.1037/emo0000376.

146 **Emotions to develop or intensify:** Smith, Ryan, William D. Killgore, and Richard D. Lane. "The Structure of Emotional Experience and Its Relation to Trait Emotional Awareness: A Theoretical Review." *Emotion* 18, no. 5 (2018): 670–92. https://doi.org/10.1037/emo0000376.

146 **With your thoughts:** University of Colorado at Boulder. "Your brain on imagination: It's a lot like reality, study shows." ScienceDaily. Accessed June 7, 2021. https:// www.sciencedaily.com/releases/2018/12/181210144943.htm.

146 **Through our behavior:** Smith, Ryan, William D. Killgore, and Richard D. Lane. "The Structure of Emotional Experience and Its Relation to Trait Emotional Awareness: A Theoretical Review." *Emotion* 18, no. 5 (2018): 670–92. https://doi.org/10.1037/emo0000376.

147 **Physical and mental health:** Rodriguez, Tori. "Negative Emotions Are Key to Well-Being." *Scientific American*, May 2013. https://www.scientificamerican.com/article/negative-emotions-key-well-being/.

148 **Intensifies emotional distress:** Ruan, Yan, Harry T. Reis, Wojciech Zareba, and Richard D. Lane. "Does Suppressing Negative Emotion Impair Subsequent Emotions? Two Experience Sampling Studies." *Motivation and Emotion* 44, no. 3 (2019): 427–35. https://doi.org/10.1007/s11031-019-09774-w.

149 **Emotional suppression over time:** Ruan, Yan, Harry T. Reis, Wojciech Zareba, and Richard D. Lane. "Does Suppressing Negative Emotion Impair Subsequent Emotions? Two Experience Sampling Studies." *Motivation and Emotion* 44, no. 3 (2019): 427–35. https://doi.org/10.1007/s11031-019-09774-w.

151 **Area of the brain associated with emotional distress:** Winerman, Lea. "Talking the Pain Away." American Psychological Association, October 2006. https://www.apa.org/monitor/oct06/talking.

154 **Describe our emotional state:** Feeling Words. Steve Hein's EQI.org. Accessed June 4, 2021. https://eqi.org/fw.htm.

159 **Internal emotional experience:** Cuncic, Arlin. "Understanding Inappropriate Affect." *Verywell Mind*, April 9, 2020. https://www.verywellmind.com/understanding-inappropriate-affect-4767992.

159 **Also lead to inappropriate affect:** Cuncic, Arlin. "Understanding Inappropriate Affect." *Verywell Mind*, April 9, 2020. https://www.verywellmind.com/understanding-inappropriate-affect-4767992.

161 **Connection is primal:** Cook, Gareth. "Why We Are Wired to Connect." *Scientific American*, October 22, 2013. https://www.scientificamerican.com/article/why-we-are-wired-to-connect/.

165 **Insomnia, and intrusive thoughts:** Raypole, Crystal. "Let It Out: Dealing With Repressed Emotions." Healthline, March 31, 2020. https://www.healthline.com/health/repressed-emotions#takeaway.

Chapter 6: How to Complain Effectively

168 **Life you want:** Hurst, Katherine. "Do You Have a 'Low' or 'High' Vibration? Read These 32 Signs." TheLawOfAttraction.com, April 8, 2021. https://www.thelawofattraction.com/low-high-vibration-read-32-signs/.

168 **Empathy in the listener:** Kowalski, Robin M. "Complaints and Complaining: Functions, Antecedents, and Consequences." *Psychological Bulletin* 119, no. 2 (1996): 179–96. https://doi.org/10.1037/0033-2909.119.2.179.

169 **What we were exposed to:** Kowalski, Robin M. "Complaints and Complaining: Functions, Antecedents, and Consequences." *Psychological Bulletin* 119, no. 2 (1996): 179–96. https://doi.org/10.1037/0033-2909.119.2.179.

170 **Annoyance about something:** Kowalski, Robin M. "Complaints and Complaining: Functions, Antecedents, and Consequences." *Psychological Bulletin* 119, no. 2 (1996): 179–96. https://doi.org/10.1037/0033-2909.119.2.179.

172 **Complaining can also become challenging:** Stillman, Jessica. "Complaining Is Terrible for You, According to Science." *Inc.,* February 29, 2016. https://www.inc.com/jessica-stillman/complaining-rewires-your-brain-for-negativity-science-says.html.

174 **Events from the previous day:** Varma, Barbara Neal. "Complaining, for Your Health." *The Atlantic,* February 8, 2015. https://www.theatlantic.com/health/archive/2015/02/complaining-for-your-health/385041/.

174 **How other people feel about us:** Kowalski, Robin M. "Complaints and Complaining: Functions, Antecedents, and Consequences." *Psychological Bulletin* 119, no. 2 (1996): 179–96. https://doi.org/10.1037/0033-2909.119.2.179.

174 **Discuss positive events:** Kowalski, Robin M. "Complaints and Complaining: Functions, Antecedents, and Consequences." *Psychological Bulletin* 119, no. 2 (1996): 179–96. https://doi.org/10.1037/0033-2909.119.2.179.

175 **People who share our complaints:** Kowalski, Robin M. "Complaints and Complaining: Functions, Antecedents, and Consequences." *Psychological Bulletin* 119, no. 2 (1996): 179–96. https://doi.org/10.1037/0033-2909.119.2.179.

175 **Reason we complain:** Kowalski, Robin M. "Complaints and Complaining: Functions, Antecedents, and Consequences." *Psychological Bulletin* 119, no. 2 (1996): 179–96. https://doi.org/10.1037/0033-2909.119.2.179.

176 **Accountable for their behavior:** Kowalski, Robin M. "Complaints and Complaining: Functions, Antecedents, and Consequences." *Psychological Bulletin* 119, no. 2 (1996): 179–96. https://doi.org/10.1037/0033-2909.119.2.179.

177 **Proposed solutions:** Varma, Barbara Neal. "Complaining, for Your Health." *The Atlantic*, February 8, 2015. https://www.theatlantic.com /health/archive/2015/02/complaining-for-your-health/385041/.

178 **Complain about the complaining:** Kowalski, Robin M. "Complaints and Complaining: Functions, Antecedents, and Consequences." *Psychological Bulletin* 119, no. 2 (1996): 179–96. https://doi.org/10.1037/0033 -2909.119.2.179.

178 **Overshadow your complaint with their own:** Kowalski, Robin M. "Complaints and Complaining: Functions, Antecedents, and Consequences." *Psychological Bulletin* 119, no. 2 (1996): 179–96. https://doi.org /10.1037/0033-2909.119.2.179.

184 **Leads to more suffering:** Cuncic, Arlin. "What Is Radical Acceptance?" *Verywell Mind*, May 26, 2021. https://www.verywellmind.com/what-is -radical-acceptance-5120614.

185 **Into a place of acceptance:** Linehan, Marsha M. *DBT Skills Training Manual.* 2nd ed. New York: Guilford Publications, 2014.

187 **Complaining is most effective:** Kowalski, Robin M., Brooke Allison, Gary W. Giumetti, Julia Turner, Elizabeth Whittaker, Laura Frazee, and Justin Stephens. "Pet Peeves and Happiness: How Do Happy People Complain?" *Journal of Social Psychology* 154, no. 4 (December 13, 2013): 278–82. https://doi.org/10.1080/00224545.2014.906380.

Chapter 7: How to Support Someone

194 **Administered by accident:** "Pain Is More Intense When Inflicted on Purpose." *Harvard Gazette*, December 18, 2008. https://news.harvard.edu /gazette/story/2008/12/pain-is-more-intense-when-inflicted-on-purpose/.

194 **Impact being the same:** Tannenbaum, Melanie. "'But I Didn't Mean It!' Why It's so Hard to Prioritize Impacts over Intents." *Scientific American*, October 14, 2013. https://blogs.scientificamerican.com/psysociety /e2809cbut-i-didne28099t-mean-ite2809d-why-ite28099s-so-hard-to -prioritize-impacts-over-intents/.

210 **Perceived threat:** Hamilton, David R. "Does Your Brain Distinguish Real from Imaginary?" Dr. David R Hamilton, PhD, October 30, 2014. https://

drdavidhamilton.com/does-your-brain-distinguish-real-from-ima
ginary/.

211 **Threatening stimuli:** Ito, Tiffany A., Jeff T. Larsen, N. Kyle Smith, and John T. Cacioppo. "Negative Information Weighs More Heavily on the Brain: The Negativity Bias in Evaluative Categorizations," *Journal of Personality and Social Psychology* 75, no. 4 (1998): 887–900. https://doi.org /10.1037/0022-3514.75.4.887.

222 **That people respond to complaints:** Kowalski, Robin M. "Complaints and Complaining: Functions, Antecedents, and Consequences." *Psychological Bulletin* 119, no. 2 (1996): 179–96. https://doi.org/10.1037/0033 -2909.119.2.179.

Chapter 8: Discrimination with a Smile

233 **Forget about everything else:** Canfield, Jack. "Using the Law of Attraction for Joy, Relationships, Money & Success." Jack Canfield: Maximizing Your Potential. Accessed June 7, 2021. https://www.jackcanfield.com/blog /using-the-law-of-attraction/.

234 **Bad for evolution:** Yakushko, Oksana. *Scientific Pollyannaism: From Inquisition to Positive Psychology.* Springer, 2019.

234 **Unhappiness of the entire society:** Yakushko, Oksana. *Scientific Pollyannaism: From Inquisition to Positive Psychology.* Springer, 2019.

235 **Name of the pursuit of happiness:** Yakushko, Oksana. *Scientific Pollyannaism: From Inquisition to Positive Psychology.* Springer, 2019.

235 **Something had to be done:** Yakushko, Oksana. *Scientific Pollyannaism: From Inquisition to Positive Psychology.* Springer, 2019.

236 **"More and more illness?":** Hicks, Esther, and Jerry Hicks. *The Law of Attraction: The Basics of the Teachings of Abraham.* 1st ed. Hay House, Inc., 2006.

236 **Our overall health:** "Determinants of Health." Office of Disease Prevention and Health Promotion, May 26, 2010. https://www.healthypeople.gov /2020/about/foundation-health-measures/Determinants-of-Health.

238 **Own mortality and health:** Ahmed, Sara. *The Promise of Happiness*. Duke University Press, 2010.

239 **Persisted throughout time:** Ahmed, Sara. "Killing Joy: Feminism and the History of Happiness." *Signs: Journal of Women in Culture and Society* 35, no. 3 (2010): 571–94. https://doi.org/10.1086/648513.

240 **Impeded the pursuit of happiness:** Yakushko, Oksana. *Scientific Pollyannaism: From Inquisition to Positive Psychology*. Springer, 2019.

240 **Threaten the overall happiness:** Yakushko, Oksana. *Scientific Pollyannaism: From Inquisition to Positive Psychology*. Springer, 2019.

242 **Happiness of the entire family:** Ahmed, Sara. *The Promise of Happiness*. Duke University Press, 2010.

243 **Liberated from the home:** Ahmed, Sara. "Killing Joy: Feminism and the History of Happiness." *Signs: Journal of Women in Culture and Society* 35, no. 3 (2010): 571–94. https://doi.org/10.1086/648513.

243 **Relieve the white woman of her burden:** Ahmed, Sara. *The Promise of Happiness*. Duke University Press, 2010.

244 **A lot to be dissatisfied with:** Ahmed, Sara. *The Promise of Happiness*. Duke University Press, 2010.

246 **Sells the promise of happiness, health, and thinness:** "How Dieting Became a $71 Billion Industry." CNBC, January 11, 2021. https://www.cnbc.com/video/2021/01/11/how-dieting-became-a-71-billion-industry-from-atkins-and-paleo-to-noom.html.

246 **"Profiting off of my insecurity?":** Marley-Henschen, Holly. "'Who Is Profiting off of My Insecurity?'" Tone Madison, March 19, 2019. https://www.tonemadison.com/articles/who-is-profiting-off-of-my-insecurity.

247 **Depression, and overall well-being:** Weingus, Leigh. "Inside the Body Image Movement That Doesn't Focus on Your Appearance." *HuffPost*, August 15, 2018. https://www.huffpost.com/entry/what-is-body-neutrality_n_5b61d8f9e4b0de86f49d31b4.

248 **Contradicted in many assessments:** Yakushko, Oksana. *Scientific Pollyannaism: From Inquisition to Positive Psychology*. Springer, 2019.

249 **Ultimately less sadness:** Kushlev, Kostadin, Elizabeth W. Dunn, and Richard E. Lucas. "Higher Income Is Associated with Less Daily Sadness

but Not More Daily Happiness." *Social Psychological and Personality Science* 6, no. 5 (2015): 483–89. https://doi.org/10.1177/1948550614568161.

250 **Result in happiness:** Ahmed, Sara. *The Promise of Happiness*. Duke University Press, 2010.

250 **You will be happy:** Ahmed, Sara. *The Promise of Happiness*. Duke University Press, 2010.

Chapter 9: How to Find Fulfillment in a Difficult World

255 **Less happy they are:** Mauss, Iris B., Craig L. Anderson, and Nicole S. Savino. "Can Wanting to Be Happy Make People Unhappy? Paradoxical Effects of Valuing Happiness." *PsycEXTRA Dataset* 11, no. 4 (August 2011): 807–15. https://doi.org/10.1037/e634112013-296.

255 **Aren't getting any happier:** Whippman, Ruth. "Americans Are Spending a Fortune on Finding Happiness—and Becoming Less Happy in the Process." *Quartz*, October 7, 2016. https://qz.com/803055/america-the-anxious-americans-are-spending-a-fortune-on-finding-happiness-and-becoming-less-happy-in-the-process/.

255 **Almost no change in American happiness:** Lush, Tamara. "Poll: Americans Are the Unhappiest They've Been in 50 Years." Associated Press, June 16, 2020. https://apnews.com/article/virus-outbreak-health-us-news-ap-top-news-racial-injustice-0f6b9be04fa0d3194401821a72665a50.

259 **Pain we are experiencing:** Zhang, Chun-Qing, Emily Leeming, Patrick Smith, Pak-Kwong Chung, Martin S. Hagger, and Steven C. Hayes. "Acceptance and Commitment Therapy for Health Behavior Change: A Contextually-Driven Approach." *Frontiers in Psychology* 8 (2018). https://doi.org/10.3389/fpsyg.2017.02350.

268 **You will not feel more motivated:** Oettingen, Gabriele. *Rethinking Positive Thinking: Inside the New Science of Motivation*. Current, 2015.

268 **Process of waiting:** Oettingen, Gabriele. *Rethinking Positive Thinking: Inside the New Science of Motivation*. Current, 2015.

268 **Explore possible avenues:** Oettingen, Gabriele. *Rethinking Positive Thinking: Inside the New Science of Motivation*. Current, 2015.

Nick Garcia

Whitney Goodman is the radically honest licensed psychotherapist behind the popular Instagram account @sitwithwhit and owner of The Collaborative Counseling Center, a private therapy practice in Miami, Florida. She helps individuals and couples heal past wounds and create the life they've always wanted. Her work has been featured in dozens of publications and programs, including the *New York Times, Teen Vogue, New York* magazine, *InStyle,* and *Good Morning America*. Whitney lives in Miami, Florida, with her husband, their son, and two dogs, Luna and Charlie.